Paleface

A Guide to Cultural Resistance in
the Age of Felonious

The author of this book is an apparently insane boxing coach and stick-fighter, who does not accept the truism that all that is wrong with the world is the fault of working class men of European descent, and that, instead, international bankers and the politicians who dance upon their puppet strings have targeted the myriad Caucasian Cultures and extant, pan-cultural notions of masculinity for extinction in an attempt to remove from the globalist path the one obstacle that might prevent the final evolution of the human race into a hive of mono-cropped primates.

Although the author is clearly insane and probably just needs to try a new flavor of stage one baby food to silence his anti-American musings, he is an entertaining crackpot. Therefore, the Council on Un-American Opinion has recommended this rampant screed as a means of ferreting out the traitors in your midst. Simply read aloud from this hate-filled rant, and should any who listen nod in agreement at any point, report them to the Council on Un-American Opinion at a University near you.

Books by James LaFond

Nonfiction

The Fighting Edge, 2000

The Logic of Steel, 2001

The First Boxers, 2011

The Gods of Boxing, 2011

All Power Fighting, 2011

When You're Food, 2011

The Lesser Angles of Our Nature, 2012

The Logic of Force, 2012

The Greatest Boxer, 2012

Take Me to Your Breeder, 2014

The Streets Have Eyes, 2014

Panhandler Nation, 2014

The Ghetto Grocer, 2014

American Fist, 2014

Don't Get Boned, 2014

Alienation Nation, 2014

In The Chinks of The Machine, 2014

How the Ghetto Got My Soul, 2014

Saving the World Sucks, 2014

Taboo You, 2014

The Fighting Life, 2014

Narco Night Train, 2014

Into the Mountains of Madness: in [3 volumes], 2014

Incubus of Your Sacred Emasculation, 2014

Breeder's Digest, 2014

The Third Eye, 2015

Modern Agonistics, 2015

By the Wine Dark Sea, 2015

The Pale Usher, 2016

The End of Masculine Time, 2015

War Drums, 2015

A Thousand Years in His Soul: The Poets, 2015

A Thousand Years in His Soul: The Seers, 2015

Of Lions and Men, 2015

Your Trojan Whorse, 2016

On Bitches, 2016

Equidistant Drowning Babies, 2015

The Boned Zone, 2015

A Sickness of the Heart: Part One, 2015

Let the Weak Fall, 2015

If I Were King, 2015

Dark Art of an Aryan Mystic, 2015

Welcome to Harm City: White Boy, 2015

When You're Food: Raw, 2016

No B.S. Boxing, 2016

Stick Fighting Fundamentals, 2016

Our Captain, 2016

Stillbirth of A Nation, 2016

America in Chains, 2106

40,000 Years from Home, 2016

The Sardonyx Stone, 2016

Neanderthal Resistance, 2016

A Dread Grace, 2016

Habitat Hoodrat, 2016

The Poor Tour/Ghetto Gourmet, 2016

40,000 Years from Home, 2016

A Once Great Medieval City, 2016

A Thousand Years in His Soul, 2016
The Liver-Eater Reader, 2016
Why Grownups Suck, 2016

Fiction

Astride the Chariot of Night, 2014
Sacrifix, 2014
Rise, 2014
Motherworld, 2014
Planet Buzzkill, 2014
Fruit of The Deceiver, 2014
Forty Hands of Night, 2014
Black and Pale, 2014
Daughters of Moros, 2014
Darkly, 2014
This Design is Called Paisley, 2015
Hurt Stoker, 2015
Poet, 2016
Triumph, 2015

Winter, 2015
The Spiral Case, 2015
Hemavore, with Dominick Mattero, 2016
Yusuf of the Dusk, 2016
Beyond the Pale, 2016
RetroGenesis: Day 1, with Erique Watson, 2015
Easy Chair, 2015
Happily Ever Under, 2015
Road Killing, 2015
Fat Girl Dancing, 2015
Buzz Bunny, 2015
T. Spoone Slickens, Inquire, 2015
Dream Flower, 2015
The Song of Jeannot, 2015
Organa, 2015
A Hoodrat Halloween, 2015
Buzz Bunny, 2015
The Consultant, 2015

Reverent Chandler, 2015
He, 2016
Little Feet Going Nowhere, 2016
DoomFawn, 2016

The Jericho Bone, 2016
Ire and Ice, 2016
Under the Crescent, 2016

Sunset Saga Novels
Big Water Blood Song, 2011
Ghosts of the Sunset World, 2011
Beyond the Ember Star, 2012
Comes the Six Winter Night, 2012
Thunder-Boy, 2012
The World is Our Widow, 2013
Behind the Sunset Veil, 2013
Den of The Ender, 2013
God's Picture Maker, 2014
Out of Time, 2015
Seven Moons Deep, 2016

For Ronald Thomas West, who offered up
direction on a road with no signposts

Contents

Paleface Sunset

The Clarity of Decline

Preface to Paleface Sunset

Paleface Sunset constitutes a six month journey into the back story of the extinction of my race. I might have arranged it as essays, resources, etc. I prefer the project to be seen for what it is, largely my response to questions from my combat, fiction and history readers who all seem to feel as if their kind of people are being phased out. One can now look in vain for a positive depiction of a white man that does not involve him submitting to the will of a woman who is wiser than he and/or saving a black person who is better than he. Two prime examples of this would be the movies Blood Diamond and Children of Men. In both cases the heroic, morally flawed, white man sacrifices himself to save a morally towering black at the behest of an insistently critical white woman.

I personally find that plot appealing and liked the variation of it in The Wild Geese, when racist, white South African mercenary fought and died to save a black politician. My problem with the above two examples—

and I did enjoy these very well made movies—is that such a plot is now a requisite for having a heroic white male lead, and that the bad guys are no longer mixed race but largely white. For instance, the Movie Tears of the Sun had realistically portrayed black villains and the movie Romeo Must Die had a scene in it in which a Chinese man unrealistically beat the piss out of an entire gang of black thugs. Neither one of these movies could be made now, 10 years or so later, in the U.S. without alterations to reflect the racial agenda of our media rulers.

Recently, I viewed the move the Equalizer, with Denzel Washington, in which all of the villains are white men. The hero is a CIA assassin who has retired and consults with his Neo Conservative female boss, a goddess dispensing death across the globe—death that is righteous and good. All of the virtues appearing in this film are held by characters that are not white, adult men, although a buffoonish white clerk is permitted a moment of nerdish glory.

If we contrast this film to the one that made Mister Washington a highly demanded A-list actor, Training Day, we see in the better, more realistic portrayal of a corrupt cop some 15 years ago, a role that would probably be rejected by any black A-list actor today, and, more importantly, would not be written. This accomplishes the twin social objectives of raising the African American man on a pedestal far too high to accommodate the fallen Caucasian, but also serves the cause of demonstrating that the only good man must be subservient to a woman or a government, otherwise his masculine expression is tainted with evil. The moviegoer can see the early evolution of this in Man on Fire, another very well made Denzel Washington movie in which his performance is excellent as he saves a white girl from her white father and white associate, in service to the white mother, with brown men dying numerous incidental deaths.

I do not like to communicate in terms of movies, as these are among our crudest cultural devices. But, for the very reason that video provides the most idiot-accessible media and the fact that postmodern opinion is almost entirely formed among the idiot masses by audio-video means, it seems to offer the most best method for determining what gender and ethnic groups are currently in favor and which are in disfavor. For instance, in 1930s films, virtually all depictions of African Americans were of jolly idiots helpful to minor white concerns. Now virtually all depictions of African Americans portray them as both superior to and mistreated by, whites. Both of these false media templates are facets of an evolving Meta-Lie. It will be fascinating to measure the tilt of this false-immensity as it spins into a future in which white men occupy the seat furthest from the throne of moral privilege.

I think it is a good vantage to occupy, for the former place of privilege held by our kind offered not a single clear view of what was to come. We are, at this point in the decline of our kind, at least advantaged with a clear understanding of our hated place in the grand scheme. I see this scheme as one purely of power, of material acquisition and generation of debt, with no true racial component. However, I believe that those who worship their own greed and imbue it with the holiness formerly reserved for faith cannot permit the men whose ancestors brought down more empires than any other two races ever raised, to continue in positions of power.

Jackal and Jill

The True Story of Neanderthal Extinction

"You'all been a piece-a-shit since the caveman days, Jack, ever since some smarter asshole came by with a sharper stick—and look at you now, out on your dumbass again and me with you!"

East Baltimore Skank screaming at Crackhead Mate, Stemmers Run and Eastern Avenue

33,000 Before Present, the Neander Valley, present day Germany

The First Man Cave

The cold lonely sky roared its displeasure above and snow poured off of his hairy thighs as he hauled the auroch haunch through the deep drifts of the valley. Brule was waiting in the Y of the small nut tree for his return. They had started the winter with only three hunters. Now they were two, and Brule had lost his strong foot fighting the auroch. He pushed all thoughts of fatigue from his mind and trudged on, the weight of the Clan's survival literally riding on his broad shoulders.

There was no time to waste. Jackal, so-named because he had been the smallest and most energetic of his age group, had to push right up the valley instead of skulking in the trees, heedless of danger, if he was going to return before the killing cold of night took Brule away to dreamtime forever. He would then carry Brule back to the cave that was their home, where Jill, Acorn-lips and the children awaited with Old Man. This haunch would feed them through the long winter nights.

Finally, there it was, up on the rise above the trees that sprouted from the valley floor, the home of the clan, the sacred resting place of their hallowed ancestors, the place First Man had taken from the cave bear, and bequeathed to all his hunter sons down through the many long winters of life.

Jackal picked up his pace, hefting his spear in his weak hand as he steadied the man-sized auroch haunch on his back with his strong arm.

His thoughts raced—well, jogged—*Jill will be so glad to see me, I know it. I shall stroke the soft fur on her broad back a few times before heading back for Brule—he will understand.*

Up through the trees he hurried, savoring the scent of wood smoke, to which would soon be added the scent of meat!

Where was Jill?

Where were Acorn-lips and the children?

If the Old Man lived he was there, for he could not move. Running now with the weight of a man on his shoulders Jackal made it up to the cave mouth, dropped the haunch and looked in to see Old Man hunched in his withered way by the fire.

"Where they?

Wolves come?"

Old Man shook his head sorrowfully and mumbled over his empty gums, "Tall ones, skinny, flying spears, take them."

Jackal wanted to run these skinny enemies down, to kill them in the night and take their women and children back. But he must retrieve Brule, so off he went, shambling along through his back trail, even snarling at a lion that barred his way, the cat shrinking back from his heavy spear of hate.

The Cave Makers

Jackal made his way through the thick snow-choked forest the day after the slaying of the auroch that took Brule's foot. The tracks were easy to follow, as there were six adult males with narrow feet and long legs, skinny fellows he could easily smash in a fight. He would smash their skulls and break their feet!

No, he would break their feet and then smash their skulls! That would be the way!

As it neared sunfall, Jackal broke through the woods at the base of the Windbottom Creek and was startled by what he saw. Along the stream was arrayed a handful—a full handful as he counted on his strong hand that was not missing the thumb—of, of caves? They were made of skins but shaped like the inside of a cave, with a cave mouth of their own which a person could crawl through. And so many narrow, elongated people were crawling through these mammoth-hide cave mouths from within their mammoth hide caves!

He saw Jill their holding two of the children, wearing some tight fitting inside-out hide with no hair on it. Why, her new attire was unseemly! She looked like some fresh woman in season!

He hefted his spear in anger and began to stalk toward his woman to reclaim her, and then a handful of long slender spears darted into the snowpack around him, thrown by the tall flat-faced twig men that stood way far back—too far to snatch and smash and break!

Jackal roared ferociously. He had grown from a jackal of a boy to a lion of a man, and it was too late. His people were gone, just lame Brule and withered Old Man back in the cave. As his angry roar faded away Jill came closer, standing under the protection of some big tall twig of a flat-faced man, and shouted, "Go away, Jack!"

"No, come to cave!"

"Jack," and she motioned to the hide caves, "we have caves any place—pretty place, many place. Go, Jack."

She looked meaningfully at the tall skinny stranger men as they took more flying spears to hand, and shouted, "Please, Jack, go!"

"I bring big auroch meat!"

"I eat much mammoth meat! Go, Jack!"

The men looked at him menacingly and he knew he must leave or die, and if he died who would feed Old Man and Brule?

Jackal walked off into the snow-choked woods as night fell, fell over the world as over his heart.

The next morning, after fighting his way through a hyena ambush and shoving his spear up a wolf's ass for sniffing him while he napped under a needle tree, Jackal made it back to the cave, where Old Man and Brule sat at the mouth, eating auroch steaks.

Brule spoke up, "Where women, children?"

Jackal snarled, "New men, narrow, elongated men, mammoth-eating men, cave-making men!"

Brule moaned in despair.

Old Man, though, had words of wisdom, "They Big Wanker Clan—took my woman. Why I come up to winter lands. Happen to us all in time."

Brule then grew less glum and suggested, "Hyenas, lions, fight, down by bone pit. Go watch?"

Jackal looked at Old Man, who answered, "Two spear points to one on lions."

Brule looked at him and accepted his wager with a laugh as Jackal lifted Old Man on his shoulders, "Hyenas rule, Old Man. Start make that spear point now!"

And they were off to watch the fights, the last of the Snow Clan, from their cave for men that stays in the same place.

'Across the Genome'

Are We the Last Neanderthals?

It is interesting that modern populations that have more of a Neanderthal contribution are more advanced in terms of mathematical scores, especially in light of their former status as the idiots of the human family tree. This lecturer does not blurt such rude observations, but does impart the information necessary to make rude observations for those of us inclined to do so.

Like all academics of our era, he veers away from violence, aggression and warfare in favor of some form of unspecified benign selection process. Of course, if he does not, he could lose his job. The possibility that humans out of Africa wiped out a larger-brained branch of our psychotic family tree does not fit with the current orthodoxy, which places Caucasian Europeans as the only genocidal aggressors on Daycare Earth. Despite the professor's setting aside of human nature, his command of the sources is broad, deep and well presented.

https://www.youtube.com/watch?v=0uRCV
yJ7-0c

Andy Yo-Clocker

Neanderthal Resistance Hall of Pain Inductee #1

What is the Neanderthal Resistance Hall of Pain?

In due time, Rock-Hoppa, in due time...

Andy is 20-years-old, five-foot eight-inches tall and 145 pounds. He is a clerk who works over night in a county supermarket, barely making ends meet and enjoying good literature like King Leer, Hamlet, Winter, and Reverent Chandler.

The night before last, on the coldest night in over a year in the Armpit of the East Coast, he was waiting for the #23 bus out to Middle River, his destination, 10 miles up the

Eastside from the busy transfer point at Charles Center: http://www.bing.com/search?q=charles+center+metro+station&form=CPDTDF&pc=CPDTDF&src=IE-SearchBox

As Andy waited in his jeans, ball cap, sweat shirt and hooded coat, a large, innocent, unarmed, black teen in his late 20s approached him and asked for a cigarette. Andy, a very friendly guy, who always asks coworkers how they are doing and cares enough to find out how they are before continuing on his way, said, "Sure, Man, here you go," and handed the bearded youth a smoke from arm's length.

Five minutes later, as Andy held his new $80 watch in the palm of his hand, the innocent, unarmed, bearded, black, teen approached again, with a second man of the same description and said, aggressively, "Give me that watch, boy!"

Andy, a scrappy fellow, said, "Okay," and slammed the watch into the mugger's face with the palm of his hand.

The mugger grabbed Andy by the collar of his coat and began lifting him and pushing him toward the wall.

Andy clinched up and threw the man with a heel-trip, landed straddled on top of the man, who was now in a fetal position and began laying in punches to the face and neck as the man laid and prayed.

Unfortunately, as Andy landed punches, his belongings were spilling out of his coat and pants pockets , clattering on the sidewalk: a $200 cell phone, his wallet with $150 in cash, his I.D. and his bus pass...

Just about as this registered in his mind, he noticed that the other innocent, unarmed, 20-something, black teen, instead of piling on as most mugging accomplices do, was scooping up his belongings!

Andy scrambled after the man with the result that both muggers fled.

Andy was screwed, with no way to bus it to work, hire a cab, or call for help.

Rather than beg, bully or steal, like most Baltimoreans who find themselves stranded on a cold night, Andy began the uphill trek to work, which took him past the main police precinct. Feeling kind of sore over the turn of events, Andy decided to do the right thing and report the crime.

On inquiring of the officer on duty Andy was informed that the victim of his unprovoked attack had already charged him with assault and battery, and that, since the victim of his violent outburst had a witness, and Andy was the suspect until proven innocent, the best he could hope for was having the case thrown out as a mutual combat. The officer declined to file a report, to seek Andy's belongings, or make a phone call to work on his behalf, reiterating to Andy, that if someone tries to take your belongings and you hit them, then you have committed an equal or greater crime and have forfeited your right to file a complaint with the police.

Hours later, Andy made it to work, but had missed his shift and was sent home, suffering further economic loss. He did not, however, whine and complain, and I had to pretty much drag this account out of him. He said, "It is what it is—can't fight the system when it's stacked against you. But I won't stop defending myself just because it's against the law."

Hang tough, Andy. The enemy may be bold, but they are weak and gutless, and one day they will not have the police to protect them. You are young yet. Perhaps you shall have the pleasure of seeing that glorious, blood-drenched day come to pass, when the police stand aside and let us Neanderthals defend ourselves against our sissy enemy.

On behalf of the readers at jameslafond.com I am presenting Andy with a black, 2014 Armitron watch which I have not been able to figure out how to set in any case.

Understanding America in 4 Conservative Sentences

Blaming the Target of Aggression: 'He Should Not Have Been Carying That Much Money'

I just had a talk with an intelligent member of my family who votes, believes in right and wrong, and thinks that there is always a way to follow lawful channels to achieve justice.

Okay, okay—stop laughing.

The funny thing is the only people who ever used to accuse the system of blaming the victim were feminists who thought it was terrible that a scantily dressed woman would be regarded as more receptive and inviting to rape.

Now, with feminists and liberals in charge that is dogma.

Sluts are sacred, nearly as sacred as hoodrats.

In a discussion with a law abiding Christian voter, she was horrified over the fate of Andy, who was attacked by two men and fought them off, but lost has wallet and cell phone, then experienced the indignity of having the police refuse to file a report and tell him to get lost and not to assault and batter any more muggers, or else.

What are the elements of this person's—a mainstream person who believes in what her government tells her—assertion, to serve as a reflection of the societal values she declares faith in, in her own words:

"He should not have had that much money on him."

This was the first thing she said and the key point of her opinion that the crime here was the taking of the money, not the act of aggression. She felt that the physical actions of Andy fighting back made this a voluntary contest and not an attack and defense, which is exactly what the media pushes down our throat—fights not attacks. The fact that a man's Autonomy was violated means almost nothing to her or society. His combat effectiveness was not commendable in her eyes or the police department's.

"That's terrible. He shouldn't have to fight. There should be more police."

The belief that the system is not corrupt and wrong but underfunded is the mainstay of human domestication and accounts for our enslavement, dependent as it is on the degenerate values of our materialistic slave cult. The use of the word should is the feminine form of submission to enslavement, with those believing that **should** belongs anywhere in a discussion of reality, real conditions and actions, exhibiting symptoms of domestication. Whenever a person uses the term should when discussing a tragedy they are fleeing in their mind into a realm of fantasy.

"He should have stayed and insisted that the police fill out a report."

The belief in the essential goodness of evil institutions is unshakable among voters who, by that very act, even if their man never gets elected, feel vested in the State institutions. This is simply genius. I retorted, "Look, he's a low income white trash guy. The cops would have beat his ass if he refused to obey their directive to leave the station."

"If he was better spoken and educated and drove this would not have happened and if it did the police would have been receptive to his complaint."

Of course, she was right on this account, which marks the everlasting victory of evil in the human mind, the form of Aristotelian confidence, that so long as the State serves the need of its rare ideal citizen it is just, and that all of those who reside outside the ideal are thus justly enslaved.

Permit me to distill this mainstream, American, Christian, conservative's statement into a functional creed for the indoctrination of young Americans.

The American Civic Creed

Do not carry cash or valuables.

Do not fight, the police will protect you.

Vote for increased police powers.

Demand that the police do your bidding.

Graduate from university with a degree and speak like it.

Do not walk or use mass transit, but buy a car and drive it.

Society will now serve your needs, citizen.

Jockstrap, Seer of the Palefaces

Recognizing The Neanderthal Resistance

About a year ago, last winter, I initiated the White Wednesday tag to aid the white nationalists in my readership with identifying articles that might interest them. Being a race traitor, yet still tolerated by my pale fellows, I thought it was the least I could do.

I would like to announce an epiphany, and also apologize for taking down the White Wednesday tag. It was pointed out to me ten months ago that if anything could get this site shutdown it would be this tag. That is not why I'm taking this tag down. Indeed, I am intent on amping up racial-oriented content.

It is just that I can't live a lie any longer.

You see, I was taking off my jock strap this morning—since my balls started falling out of my body people have been calling me jockstrap—and I don't go anywhere without one.

Twenty minutes ago, as I looked down to assess the damage from last night's shift, I looked at this rather funky—oft sweated through jockstrap, which I wash out in hot water and occasionally peroxide every day. Looking at this barely white supporter of the wreckage that was once a means of dominance and a weapon of terror that threatened the world with my genetic perpetuation, I had to conclude, that no part of me, other than the whites of my eyes, are white. Even the off-white of this garment shone like 20 bond glossy Hammermill paper next to my legs.

Call me Aryan, Indo-European, Caucasian, if you will, but white is entirely inaccurate and hyperbolic, a flash image once used to wow the dim minds of colonial slaves into believing that the pale face that was fucking them was part divinity.

If I might compress a quarter-million years into a paragraph: For hundreds of thousands of years mankind developed along three paths, the African, the Neanderthal and the Disnovian. 74,000 years ago the Toba Super Eruption occurred, causing a six-year nuclear winter, which wiped out all but a couple thousand lucky Africans. I don't know anything about the Disnovians. I do know that the Neanderthals across Europe and North Asia took the nuclear winter in stride, as they were cold-adapted. By 70,000-40,000 years ago one particular group of Africans produced some killer genius whose genes are in us all. The Neanderthals were wiped out soon thereafter at the peak of a nasty ice age that they were best suited to deal with. They were murdered.

Interestingly enough:

Neanderthals showed the first signs of a spiritual life.

It was not until they wiped out the Neanderthals—interbreeding with enough of them to leave a Neanderthal trace in the genome of between 2-6% in Caucasians, Asians and American Indians—that the only surviving branch of humanity, the Africans, began showing signs of a spiritual life.

Since that time those populations with Neanderthal DNA have founded every major religion, have discovered every main entry science law and consistently field the top finishers in mathematics [I thing Peruvians and North Asians have a lock on this].

Now, after spending a life wondering about "cavemen" and Neanderthals, and being repeatedly referred to in those terms by the one segment of humanity who, in America, seem bent on beating and killing as many people with N-DNA as possible, I have decided to come out of the cave—I'm an N-DNA Carrier, a Neanderthal, if but barely. Chinese are the only groups attacked more than Europeans, and they are the only group with more N-DNA.

Call me superstitious, call me a paranoid, Jockstrap Paleface, but I suspect that there might be an unconscious drive on the part of much of humanity—even including many N-DNA carriers—to strive for the eradication of N-DNA carriers.

White, in our End Time has become synonymous with weakness, guilt, privilege, fear and the envy, imitation and worship of melanin-rich people.

Being white used to mean sitting at home safely while bully cops beat the shit out of other people as a warning not to mess with whitey.

Well whitey doesn't own the cops anymore and the ripe fruit he has become is being picked, so I am content to be an N-DNA Carrier and Resister.

Henceforth I regard white as an insult.

I'm a paleface N-DNA Carrier dedicated to bringing attention to the plight of My Kind in the form of the Neanderthal Resistance Hall of Pain, recognizing and glorifying defiance against those tasked with rubbing us out, as well as their masters.

I am proud to be a Neanderthal.

Rain on My Knuckle-Dragging Parade?

Tackling Timmy: Addendum to Jockstrap, Seer of the Palefaces

Yes, I understand Neanderthals had short arms...

When I played football for Trinity Middle School, in Washington, PA, as as a not-so-tight end, I had two guys I hit a lot, as soon as I dealt with the fat dude in front of me: the pretty quarterback, who was white, and Timmy Lipscomb, probably the nicest guy in school, a black kid, all muscle. As a virulent race traitor I loved hitting Pretty Boy and felt guilty about hurting Timmy. Once, in a mid-December scrimmage, I hit Timmy so hard I thought he was dead. But the dude never, ever gave up the ball. He was laying on the ground shivering, his arms apparently frozen around the ball in about 10 degrees. Rick and I picked him up and he did not bend, but tilted upright like a fencepost—that's when we noticed he was a gray white color, his skin splitting and chaffing into white flakes—I having hit Timmy so hard he turned white!

In any case, I stopped following Neanderthal research in 2013, and the jury is a long way—if ever—from coming in on the mapping of their genome. Bone analysis of their diet though is remarkably thorough. There is also the issue of regional variation. What makes us think that every Neanderthal from France, to Palestine, to Siberia was one color? In paleoanthropology each generation—and now each team—of researchers seems to offer an overarching all or nothing, monolithic theory for this or that. We can spend a lifetime with these geeks via the link below.

http://www.bing.com/search?q=paleoanthropology+podcasts&form=CPDTDF&pc=CPDTDF&src=IE-SearchBox

Since the post *Jockstrap, Seer Of The Palefaces* I have received some interesting facts and opinions, links and e-mails, and am thrilled—and do not worry, as a true crackpot I will bend whatever contrary information you send to my single-minded purpose!

Some—maybe all—Neanderthals were dark-skinned, you say?

So was Timmy until he got hit by that polar bear. Besides, I am not hung up on genetics, but on the human spirit, the spun fabric of ideas that forms the collective and divisive mind.

They committed genocide?

Amen, Brother, amen!

Genocide is underrated. If you don't think so, consider, when was the last time a Canaanite or a Tasmanian broke into your car?

If we only have paternal genetic markers from Neanderthals, than that is all the better—we domesticated moderns having quite enough bitch in us already—and bolsters my contention that the Neanderthal mind was the font of modern human spirituality.

That Neanderthals were cannibals—at least some of the time—has been clear for decades. So were the Aztecs, one of the most spiritually obsessed people in history. Catholicism is predicated on the metaphoric devouring of the body and blood of Christ—and for the duration of the high Middle Ages it was thought that the holy wafers and wine were actually the body and blood of Christ! Jewish bakers were routinely killed for molesting the wafers! In Moby Dick, the most spiritual Character is Queequeg the cannibal. My favorite Retro-Neanderthal, Liver-Eating Johnson, was a renowned cannibal.

Even if there is no link between myself and the Neanderthals other than the fact that their ancestral lands were mine in another age, and that they dreamed of something other than the mechanics of fueling and pleasuring the human body, in contrast to the majority of humanity today and of the modern homo sapiens who wiped them out, that is enough for me.

Of my uncles the two I treasure the most as guiding lights are Uncle Robert [a genius crackpot quadroon] and Uncle Herb, who also married into the family, and discussed literature with me, lending me the books he read while working as an engineer in the Merchant Marine. The men that mated with my aunts were better men than the ones related to my parents through blood.

Even if the Neanderthals, who I like to think were my distance partial ancestors, merely inspired me to deal with our current Spiritual Ice Age as they did with their physical one, than I'm still Jockstrap, Seer of the Palefaces [and that I am], and Feral Neanderthal.

Please, keep your information and opinions coming on this subject, which has fascinated me since childhood, and which got me kicked out of history class for arguing with the teacher over the Bearing Land Bridge theory, which I always thought was stupid, as the Native Americans probably used skin boats rather than trek across ice melt mires recently scraped to the bone by retreating glaciers. I am looking forward to the Neanderthal Resistance discussion being a learning experience for me.

I'm feeling cavemanish this evening, still pumped up from putting down a prime buck stick-fighter and also disarming him once—and thankfully unable to recall the five rounds I got smoked in, because my head is still ringing—or is that the moon calling down to me in the murky mist of night with her sweet song?

'Matriarchal Neanderthals?'

'Really, James?': A Man Question from Al

"James, I dig your extreme masculinity stance, and your primal view. But, I was reading Pillages of Time, and noticed that your Neanderthals have this quasi-matriarchal family structure. Matriarchal Neanderthals? Really James? What the hell, guy?"

-Al

Okay Al, I do not believe in time travel, yet have written 11 time travel novels. It is a mental exercise, bro. I write from the point of view of as many different character types as possible. When it comes to science-fiction I am not an advocate for this theory or that, but essentially an adventure writer who wants to do action with character depth and is willing to experiment with any sci-fi theory.

Personally, if I had to bet, I would guess that the Neanderthals were patriarchal. But, hey, Bro, what's left of them is quite matriarchal, don't you think? Look around at all of these sissy boys!

Why did I decide on a matriarchal structure for the Neanderthals in Beyond the Ember Star? *Beyond The Ember Star In Print*

First, you may not know, that five novels later in Den of the Ender I went with a patriarchal Neanderthal family structure.

Ghost Walker

I went with a Neanderthal social structure in Europe that was pseudo-matriarchal because of the following reasons:

1. Neanderthals picked flowers and used them in burial rites [not a dude's job, so I would argue for female shaman]

2. From the evidence of only one antler used to record the lunar cycle, I reckoned that Homo Neanderthalis was concerned with menstrual cycles [something only a hen-pecked dude is worried about]

3. Cave habitation was prominent, and the life in caves, I thought, might argue for a womb-oriented theology, rather than a rain [cock and balls] oriented theology.

4. Evidence I saw in 2011 suggested a low birthrate among Neanderthal women, which increases reproductive value in a community without missile weapons when you are playing the Green Bay Packers with four legs and horns against harp sticks every Sunday just to put meat on the spit. They mostly ate rodeo bulls and had to kill them with hand weapons.

5. I owe Michael Crichton for the first inkling that Neanderthals might have been matriarchal, from his book Eaters of the Dead, in which he attributes the legend of Beowulf to a memory of remnant Neanderthals eating modern humans in the Nordic lands.

6. If we find out that our remnant Neanderthal DNA is matrilineal then it points the finger at Neanderthal women for having left their men for the guys with the better tool kit.

If you want to know what I really think happened to Neanderthals read *Jackal And Jill*.

What Are You?'

A Conversation with S.J. on Race and Identity

"For forty years I've been involved with black men in basketball, karate and business. I have known really great guys like Marc, Rocky—liberal intellectuals like Brad and this kid I used to teach who now lives in Paris and has a black power radio show— and a whole bunch of knuckle-draggers and scumbags. Hell, I was a hippie, believed black men were heroes and that Nixon was the Devil back in nineteen-seventy-two— even got shot defending a black guy from some Italian monstrosity.

"Most of my students have been black. Probably my best moment as a teacher came twenty years ago, instructing at Shabumi. A racist, black Muslim woman, who I knew hated me because of the color of my skin, watched me teach a class and then approached me. I thought I was in for it, about to get vilified for making black kids do pushups. She told me that I was an excellent teacher. It's nice to get an unfiltered compliment like that. It made me work harder. Now, I know nothing about the women—I leave it to you to plumb the mysteries of African American womanhood.

"There are only two things that I have noticed about black American men—other than the propensity for violent crime— that really bothers me and I have seen it in every single one of them:

"One, every black man I have every known has regarded it as a sacred duty to have sex with as many women as possible. I've known white guys who were unfaithful to their women. I have never been unfaithful to a woman, and do not agree with it, but do understand it. But this idea that you absolutely have to try and have sex with every woman you come into contact with is simply beyond my comprehension. I am currently teaching with Rodney [his assistant], a really super church-going guy. I could not imagine him cheating on his wife, and am hoping he will be the first black guy to answer following question from a none-racial perspective.

"Two, and most disturbing. When I ask a white man, 'Are you a man who happens to be white, or are you a white person who happens to be a man,' they will mostly choose to identify themselves as a person first, and by their race second, if that. Asking that same question to black men every single one of them has answered that they are black first and a human being second, that before they are a human being they are a member of a race, as if they are some kind of bacterial spore.

"Personally, as long as blacks and other groups see themselves as members of their race first, and human second, I don't see any hope for addressing the problems with our society, particularly the problems with blacks, who commit most of the violent crime. Do you realize that if we suddenly had no black people in this city that crime would evaporate, that we would go from three-hundred and forty-odd murders to three?

"What are your thoughts on that, Mister Jim? You seem to be the internet voice of disenfranchised white men. Why do white men see themselves first and foremost as human beings and blacks see themselves first and foremost as black?"

James' Response

I believe I am a man first and a racial vector second, and [black] Brad believes he is a racial vector first and a man second, because we are both slaves to the same liberal master and according to our different functions are bound to the same vast lie that is civilization, specifically the unique experiment of American Civilization.

When England first colonized North America in the 1600s, and relied on Indians to keep their white and black slaves on the plantation, they did not want the white slaves to identify themselves as English, or

Scottish or Irish, but as bond-men, just as the blacks were merely bond-men.

From 1674-82 there was a series of combined white /black slave revolts [one was white, black and red], which convinced the ruling class to increase the number of blacks [who were vastly outnumbered by the whites] and begin handling each population according to separate terms in order to play them off against each other.

In the 1750s, with increased Indian hostilities, it was found necessary to arm the white servant class. Once this was done they had to be directed away from the plantations and toward the Indians. At this point, it was increasingly difficult to employ poor whites to eradicate Indians in order to obtain more resources and also serve as slave-catchers of runaway blacks, without playing to their racial identity.

Previously, in most societies, it was normal for only a minority of the members of any nation to identify with the nation. The Spartans and Athenians were outnumbered 10 to 1 by slaves and resident "stranger friends." The Aztecs and Incas were vastly outnumbered by subject ethnic groups, which contributed to their downfall against the Spanish.

There are various ways of addressing this problem, such as displacing peoples and forcing them to migrate to areas where they will be culturally out of place, such as the Incas and the Assyrian did regularly.

Romans were vastly outnumbered by their slaves while their Empire was growing. The Imperium stagnated when so many of the conquered peoples obtained citizenship that most of the subjects of Rome were "Romans." After this happened you see Roman officials employing gladiators [warrior slaves] as security forces and emperors employing foreign mercenaries as main force military units.

Other empires—such as the ancient Egyptians who employed black police, the Ottomons who employed Christian slave soldiers in the form of the Janissaries, the Byzantines who employed Norse mercenaries, and now the New York City

Police department, which is actively recruiting immigrant officers from Africa, Latin America and the Middle East—have utilized foreign law enforcers who will lack empathy for the population in order to see the will of the State done.

In 1800s America, with the extermination or subjugation of hundreds of Amerindian tribes by racially motivated poor white men, the United States had a vast land—nearly a continent—to domesticate and cultivate. This was established in unbelievably short order—a mere two generations—by racially motivated and entitled men and women who believed, for perhaps the first time in human history, that the State was an instrument of their will, rather the normal relationship that has typified man's relationship with the State as its servitor.

Having achieved its greatest territorial extent with the Spanish American War the United States no longer had—as an entity of subjugation—fresh conquests against which to direct racially identified whites of the lower classes—which is to say most whites. Therefore the 1900s saw the gradual erosion of white identity, as a strong white identity could now only threaten the State. The fact that the failed German effort to dominate Europe was pursued with overt white identity overtones, and that this feature of the conflict was cultivated into the dominant narrative, insured that the moral sustainability of any white identity movement would be weak.

White identity politics were abandoned by the U.S. Government as a tool which task was in the past. Rather a generic "American" identity, to be shared by all, was proposed in the interim. As soon as this was accomplished the government of the United States gradually put all of its weight behind advancing the cause of racial animosity. The three mechanism for this were (1) an infliction of white guilt to undermine any form of racial solidarity among the majority white population, (2) a fanning of a spirit of violent racial entitlement among the minority black population, and (3) the importation and neglect to assimilate people from nations that have been victimized by the U.S., insuring that the majority white population will be hemmed in by unsympathetic groups, just as the Roman citizen of the late empire was at the mercy of the urban mob and the rural barbarian immigrants.

In summation, whites see themselves as American or people first and whites only in extremis, because this best serves the interest of the State by weakening solidarity among its majority subjects.

Likewise, blacks see themselves as blacks first and Americans second, because this best serves the interest of the State, in terms of cultivating an aggressive mob population large enough to threaten the unarmed white majority, but not vast enough to in any way threaten the State itself.

Finally, the importation of vast numbers of people who do not identify themselves as human or American first, but according to various foreign perspectives, puts a varied and potent tribal toolkit in the hands of the State, which will be able to mobilize auxiliary threats to the white majority in rural areas where black mobs function poorly if at all, and at levels of social sophistication where the urban mob is found wanting, such as in the media and academia, and ultimately as a check on black America, which stands as the most disposable segment of the population in the long run.

In my opinion the American State, as the entity is currently evolving, will be most sustainable as an information plantation for the continued domestication of humans, if it has a population that breaks down as follows according to form and function.

Majority: White,   40%, production/consumption

Minority: Latino,   30%, production/consumption

Vested Auxiliary: Black, 15%, threat, redistribution

*Non-vested Majority: Islamic, 10%, threat, redistribution

Specialized Auxiliary: 5%, management

*Dependence on this type of force provider was one of the military factors that sunk the Roman Empire, as well as medieval Egypt.

Frying Pan Justice

A Neanderthal Resistance Report from Mescaline Franklin

"A man (and two women!) fighting back, they must have read your analysis of Colin Flaherty's book."

We will increasingly see news of such attacks away from major media markets. People who foil attacks in criminally permissive places like Baltimore, D.C. and Detroit, and in the leviathan cities like LA, Chicago and New York will either not report the incident for fear of becoming a target of the media and state, or their taking care of business will not be reported so as to preserve the tenor of the Victimocracy.

We will also see increasing numbers of injured home invaders bringing charges of racism and excessive force.

Way to go!

By the way, the best type of blunt kitchen weapon is the cast iron omlete skillet. Use it end-on against the neck and collar bone of a skinny dude or into the ear of a big dude. Remember to chop, not swing, keeping continuity between your body and elbow until the last instant. Become a Neanderthal gourmet and invest in cast iron cookware!

http://abc11.com/news/fayetteville-intruder-gets-a-little-frying-pan-justice/1161315/

Neanderthal Idiots in Harm City

Sympathy for the Devil... But None for White Victims of Violence By Colin Flaherty

The story here from Colin Flaherty and a Baltimorean who recently moved away because he made the idiot mistake of saving a black woman from her bat wielding boyfriend, is sobering in a pathetic way. The discussion is about a tragic and unreported murder of a white man by a black punk on his front porch, where he heroically put his wife and daughter into extreme danger by abandoning all masculine and familial responsibility and trying to save a hate-filled people from themselves.

Where did this idiot Neanderthal move to? Herring Run Park [facing it rather, the white guys who live in Herring Run Park do not have wives.] Here is a brief list of items that I have experienced walking through that park and just beyond to the bus stop:

1. 2 men board the bus I am on, and begin shooting at a guy seated in front of me, who runs off the back with them on his tail

2. An innocent unarmed black youth shot at me with a 25 auto from the sidewalk of the park, the three rounds impacting the bus frame below where I was sitting on the back right side of the #15 bus

3. 2 youths trailed me through the park and waited outside the liquor store for me while I purchased my weapon. When I exited, smacking the 22 oz bottle into my left palm, they retreated

4. A large black man stepped out of a doorway and screamed into my face, "Give me money!" I told him that I had 617 dollars in my wallet and he declined to try and take it from me as I palmed my razor.

5. A Vietnamese lady friend of mine was tortured while handcuffed by a black cop at her father's grocery 200 yards from this park.

6. 2 youths followed me into the park, where I turned on them with a foot long knife. After they fled I used the knife to make a spear I could hide there.

7. Duz, total tough guy, a Polish dude who only dates black women, and has been run over by black gunmen in a stolen car, and just shrugged it off, moved out of that neighborhood 20 years ago because his house got broken into every time he left it.

8. Black men from this neighborhood gather in packs and raid neighboring areas.

That is just a sampling of my own experiences in that location. My 40 year old female cousin was mugged there by two innocent unarmed black youths. My 18-year-old female cousin was raped on the street corner right there by an innocent unarmed black youth wielding a knife.

These yuppie "blockbuster" musicians, who think they can save those who hate them and put their women and children in danger to assuage their own misplaced feminist guilt and world-saving bitch complex, should be staked out, skinned, have their eyelids pinned back, and left for the crows.

I am not sorry that man was killed by my enemies while he was in the process of helping them.

I have no compassion for the slain man, or his world-saving friend who has since fled to the Left Coast.

I might add that I like this park and have used it for the setting of numerous stories and novels, including Buzz Bunny. My five year old son once caught a frog here while I stood over him with a bowie knife strapped to my leg.

And you move your wife and daughter right into the middle of Indian Country, and not just any Indian Country, but Black Feet hunting grounds?

Die fool, die.

Read   more:
http://www.americanthinker.com/articles/2
016/01/sympathy_for_the_devil_but_none_f
or_white_victims_of_violence.html#ixzz3y5O
RkdBG

Follow us: @AmericanThinker on Twitter |
AmericanThinker on Facebook

'Ain't No Fun When the Rabbit Got the Gun'

Barbarism and Civilization: An Experiment in Pedestrian Investigation

Yesterday, with two feet of snow against my window, I was reading Robert E. Howard's Sword Woman and other Historical Adventures. In the introduction by Scott Oden, which was very well done, he began discussing Howard's view of civilization, quoting Howard from Beyond the Black River, in many ways one of his best tales:

"Barbarism is the natural state of mankind...civilization is un-natural. It is the whim of circumstance. And barbarism must always ultimately triumph."

Of course, every natural disaster and every war and lesser natural event that brings to a halt the promised rescue of each of us by our increasingly maternalistic Civilization, gives us a taste of barbarism, of a life lived without the immediacy of the threat of punishment and promise of physical salvation that is Civilization.

With the north wind no longer blowing my way, I decided to take a late afternoon walk, six miles northwest, over three gentle ridgelines, to Towson, where my youngest son has just settled on a house a couple miles north of the city line. In case of a true disaster or social breakdown he is among the handful of people I have committed to checking in on. I would also like to time my walk. More importantly, I would like to see the true composition of the neighborhood along the route and on both ends, his and mine. The fact is, those who are normally seen on the street in urban areas are not those who live there, but service industry employees, like myself, passing through and criminals, diligently scouting for easy prey. The walk is in three stages.

Stage 1: 3 p.m.

Heading northwest out of Hamilton into Parkville I stay south of the city line for two miles. In Hamilton we have hipster and yuppie men digging out, two actual breeding white families, and a number of black women. There is not a brutha in sight, none.

On Harford Road I pass a cute little snow bunny, a 4 foot 10 inch redheaded hooker, heroically trying to sell her ass, in beany hat, beany gloves and soggy beany decorating her knit leg warmers. She is about 18, one of the daughters of the affluent from Harford County, recently immigrated from the paradise to which her parent's fled, come to Harm City in search of cheaper drug prices, lower rent and more men willing to debase her.

A half mile out I see a police car cruising with his lights on, which is the "proactive presence" style of patrolling in vogue among swine kind these days. The primary roads are 1.5 lanes on each side. The secondary streets are 1.25 lanes wide, and the side streets are snow drifts, where people either leave their vehicle buried or hopefully cut out a snow free space around it hoping that they get ploughed "out" and not "in."

Heading out Old Harford Road I see a BT-1200 coming my way, walking with traffic, in the center of her half lane and trusting to her servants and worshippers to go around her. I stand aside and let the cars pass.

I pass two single hipsters and one black homeowner digging out, all three of them saying hello, none of them being men I have previously seen while walking this street.

Further up the street I pass a wide old property, a former mansion now occupied by two middle class blacks in their mid thirties. The frontage of the sidewalk is sixty yards! The snow is a hard three feet deep, having been ploughed up from a powdery 29 inches into a wall. They have started on opposite ends of the property front digging out the sidewalk and heaving the snow over the fence into the large yard. [Granted, I have no way of knowing if they both started at the same time.] He, started at the far edge of the property and stood three yards in, leaning on his shovel, breathing deep and mopping a sweating brow with his knit hat as he mumbled to himself. She had begun at the driveway and stood, a statuesque example of African American womanhood, at about six feet tall with an elongated hourglass figure terminating—as far as this discerning eye could tell due to the snow bank—in what Richard Burton would have surely called "a stupendous buttocks!"

From beneath the rim of her black felt beret she looked on her man with disgust—a fine picture of agrarian maternity in her tight black jeans and black bunny jacket with the fur cuffs and collar—who could have surely ploughed, sown, reaped and threshed enough grain to feed Jared Taylor's entire extended family way back in the day! Noticing my admiration of her hind parts she batted her eye lids at me, smiled demurely, then looked angrily at her man, gave a silent snarl, and chopped into the intervening wall of snow with her trusty shovel.

Crossing Northern Parkway I pass two more white men and a black woman digging out, and then, looking to my left, come face-to-face with a red-headed babe in her mid twenties who was as tall as the top of the line BT-1000 that I was previously admiring, but prettier, and proportioned along the lines that my modern homo sapien friends find more appealing. I would say that she was six foot and 160. She greeted me with a wide, surprised smile as she straightened up with a shovel full of snow like she was having all of the fun in the world and said, in a thick Eastern European accent, "Hello!"

I said, "Good afternoon," and declined to stay and chat. She did intrigue me though. Is she a Russian slave girl sent outside by her madam to shovel snow so that her pimp can pick her up and take her down town to the Hyatt Regency? Is she an internet bride, acquired by some lucky local guy from the land of lucidly fuckable Caucasian babes that Manuel described in that recent podcast on SingleDudeTravel.com?

Finally, in an area in which only pairs and trios of innocent unarmed black youth are normally out and about, I saw two large black teenagers out with snow shovels, making the rounds, offering to shovel snow for residents. Old Harford Road on this stretch had not been ploughed, so I cut west into the residential area on the city line.

Stage 2: 3:30 p.m.

Southwestern Parkville sits on a ridgeline running from the southwest to the northeast, and separates the typical grid sprawl of Parkville Proper with a corridor built around Perring Parkway, a wide boulevard that is not part of the old grid, and is dotted with parks, upscale developments and prefabricated ghettos on the east side where the shopping center is. Coming up behind this shopping center on foot at night is normally a dicey proposition with hoodrats on the prowl out of the notorious Dutch Village Apartments, where numerous murders of non-gang victims, stompings, _She's So C-c-cold!_, and a rash of recent stabbings have occurred since I have been traversing the area regularly over the past 10 years.

In an area that has no foot traffic most of the time, occasionally traversed by the honest pedestrian or prowling hoodrats, I find myself walking through a mixed-race hive of homeowner worker bees. As it turns out the residents are half white half black and all friendly, with the problems in the neighborhood coming from outsiders from Wet Baltimore who use the black population as a cover and come hunting, and the youths from the section-eight friendly Dutch Village Apartments looming only a hundred yards away behind the shopping center.

I cross the shopping center access ramp where two black fellows, father and son, dig out their work truck and car and give a friendly word to me and another passing Neanderthal.

Jogging across Perring Parkway, I access the base of Oakliegh, which is a secondary street that runs diagonal to the usual grid from the Loch Raven Reservoir down to this last ghetto outpost of Baltimore, where it bleeds over the county line.

I pass a trio of large women muscling a van out of a snow bank: large, jolly, intimidating, and in three generations BT-800, BT-1000 and the just off the line BT-1200! Just in case the three bears are hungry, old Silver Locks darts around them gingerly and picks up his pace.

Walking through the area behind the Jewish cemetery I feel like I am in the countryside further north. I then come to Pappas Restaurant and Bar where the owner was recently pistol-whipped in brutal fashion by a West Baltimore thug. Here, a middle-aged black couple pull up in a car to see if the bar is open, just as a large grizzled Neanderthal drunk I know from the Raven Inn out on Loch Raven walks up and inquires if they are open. They have a friendly "gosh darn, where can I get a drink" conversation, as I cross Taylor Avenue.

Stage 3: 4.pm.

As I cross Taylor I leave the mile deep City-County buffer that the Towson Precinct of the Baltimore County Police are trying hard to hold against the invading hoodrats—who are nevertheless winning the battle of attrition, as they are being dropped in behind the lines by the City Housing Authority buying houses and renting them for section-8 vouchers. The terrain—with no sidewalk and no bus route—is now firmly old suburban, not the new hoodrat-friendly suburban sidewalk grid that has been installed since my childhood. The people shoveling out are seven Neanderthal to one black, single family homes dominating the roadway, with one apartment complex, but without bus access and not on a walk through grid. In fact, this neighborhood is difficult to drive through from east to west as the roads cut back and dead end, causing the low energy output hoodrat raiding parties to bypass it like mechanized invaders skirting a swamp.

As I near my destination a gigantic black man approaches me, dragging a snow shovel behind him. He is sixty years old, and wanted to know, "Are you good, brother? You need anything I'm here to help. Name's Samson, you can call me Sam."

We shook hands, mine disappearing in his.

"Thanks, no. I just walked out from the city to visit a friend and check out my son's new place."

"Oh, it's all good out here—that's why I moved out the way. Can't deal with that mess in town no more. Just out and about makin' sure the neighbors are all good. What about back the way, any trouble?"

"You know what, I only saw one cop, but not a single punk in sight, nothing but men and some women digging out. A couple good boys making the rounds with a snow shovel."

Samson grinned, patted his shovel, and nodded left and right to the men out shoveling, "Ain't no fun when the rabbit got the gun! Is it brother?"

"No, sir."

"You have a nice safe day now, sir."

Civilization and Barbarism

And we were off on our separate uncivilized ways, bringing me to think about what comes to mind every time I read Howard's old claims that Barbarism was natural and decent, the seat of strength, honor, courage and self-reliance, and that Civilization is its opposite, whimsical and corrupt, the seat of weakness, dishonor, cowardice and dependence.

I thought further, back two years, to my training session with the lead instructor for the Baltimore Country Guardian Angels, a group of decent, non-criminal men who simply want to discourage crime through a group presence, a group who has been forbidden to patrol on pain of arrest by the Baltimore County Police Department, the same police department that completely abandoned Essex, Rosedale and Middle River to armed black mobs who hunted us Neanderthals with impunity for a week, while diverting all resources to protecting the slim corridor of affluent whites in Towson, where I now walked.

My youngest son is soon moving from Middle River to Towson, this outpost of the affluent. At least I know, that when the looting that is going on down town [You will not hear about it but the tactical squad with their bat mobile and the chopper have been down there keeping a lid on it as I made my own unsuccessful bid to get across town to Middle River on the bus tonight and returned on foot.] tonight, and has not abated clear out to the North Baltimore City line since last April's riots and purge, heads out to Glen's new house, that I'm an hour away, and that there are a lot of men between him and the enemy **if** the agents of Civilization permit them to defend themselves.

Civilization, our most advanced social contract, rests on the surety that the individual gives what is asked by the State, and, in return, that the State protects the individual and his property, or at least avenges their loss. Recently, across America, and most glaringly in Baltimore, the State has failed—declined, even—to fulfill its end of the contract, and has at the same time become more stridently jealous of its monopoly of force, insisting, with ever more resolve, that the individual should accept injury and loss—with fear of death being the only justification for the use of force on the part of the individual—and seek redress via the State at a later time.

After four decades of reading on primitive societies, I have only found two mentions of predation within the tribe, and both of these were in highly stressed groups that had been under pressure by Civilization to the point of social collapse and began acting as gangs. Gangs are absolutely not a feature of tribal life, but are the puss of Civilization, a violent reaction of the collective human mind to the faceless savagery and tyranny of Civilization. A gang can never defeat a tribe, nor will a tribe tolerate a gang. Yet in our sick society the tribal facade left to us is this, the gang, the punk pecking order of bitch-raised man-boys who always betray each other in the face of the enemy, for they suffer most acutely from the sickness of Civilization.

"Ain't no fun when the rabbit got the gun."

What Samson said so succinctly was that those who believe in Civilization, and live according to its rules represent the rabbits, with law enforcement representing the licensed hunter and game wardens, and criminals representing the poacher. If you do not believe this, try forming a neighborhood militia and you will find the police and the criminals cooperatively in league against you.

The specific sickness of Civilization can best be understood by looking at Barbarism.

The strength of the primitive, the primal, the barbaric, is that such cultures envision the natural world as predominantly male in nature, the father that sends his son off into the world, trusting to the life and wits breathed into him to survive and prevail.

Thus is the weakness of Civilization exposed, for Civilization is the mother that keeps us close, coddles us, and does not let us fight one another or defend ourselves, but does it for us.

Civilization is matriarchy.

The place for the mother is at birth and in childhood.

Permitting motherhood over male youth is the death of manhood.

Permitting Civilization stewardship over man is the death of humanity.

Never have I been more certain that Man's present coddled course, suffused in the material glut of an inauthentic lifeway, must end in either a deserved oblivion or the accursed female hive.

Afterward

My nocturnal jaunts along the same route, over the intervening two nights since, were just as barren of predators, and quite serene, a slice of wilderness life granted to the urban dweller, the carved out driveways giving the houses the appearance of old homesteads under the streetlight-like moon that shined pale and metallic. Also, my walking time was under an hour between 4 and 5 a.m. with no traffic to deal with.

'The Angel of Death Has Spoken'

Eaters of the Dead by Michael Crichton, Illustrated by Ian Miller

1976, Bantam Books, 217 pages

For anyone that has researched the Norse, the brief fragment of Ibn Fadlan from A. D. 922 describing a Norse funeral in Russia, in which a slave girl is inseminated by the foremost men and then sacrificed by The Angel of Death, an old shamanic crone, leaves a lasting impression. I read it when I was 14, at about the time this novel was written. This passage and the few associated observations were used in the first season of the cable series The Vikings, and also served Michael Crichton in his off beat exploration of two European questions:

Who were "the little people" who figure so prominently in legend as dwarves, elves, leprechauns, pixies, kobolds, goblins and brownies?

Crichton answers this question with the other huge European origins question, The Neanderthals.

He does so by tying in the historical observations of Ibn Fadlan and the saga of Beowulf. All along he commits to the fiction that there is a complete account of Fadlan's manuscript and names various cleverly contrived bogus sources, until finally he lets the reader of the hook by naming the Necronomicon by H.P. Lovecraft as a source. The footnotes are predominantly nonfiction and informative.

The author does present a clear picture of the depths of slavery in Arabic and Norse culture. Indeed the word slave derives from the Arabic term for the Slavic girls they bought from Rus slave raiders.

As a Neanderthal-identified reader I quite liked the following line from a Norseman to

Ibn Fadlan, "You Arabs are like old women, you tremble at the sight of life."

The illustrations by Ian Miller are perfectly harsh and ritualistic in tone.

If you can't get a hold of the book, try the movie The Thirteenth Warrior, with Antonio Banderas.

'Who Built This Place?'

The Dark Lords of Hattusha

© 2016 James LaFond

From the BBC, curators of the ancient world, comes the best documentary I have seen in a while. The Hittites proved important to my study of the origins of ancient boxing, and long dead geeks like Binkler made my bookwork possible. What makes an excellent documentary on extinct civilizations is the weaving in of the story behind the discovery of said civilization. A hundred and more years ago discovery was an adventure, not merely a discussion of the material discovered by others.

As to the theories concerning the location of the Hittite capital, their power was in iron, found in their homeland. There was also the question of the Sea Peoples, among them the

Philistines, the Sickels and Danyen, who, according to the Egyptions, "where in their isles." Despite the precautions of the Hittites to keep their centers of power beyond easy reach of the sea, did not help them on the battlefield. The Sea Peoples were like the Vikings of the ancient world, fast Vikings, runners who ran up into the back of the Egyptian, Hittite, Assyrian and Cretan chariots.

Just like the Chinese Great Wall, the Maginot Line, Tyre, and the seven-walled city of Constantinople, upon which J.R.R Tolkien based the principal city of Gondor in The Lord of the Rings, an impregnable fortress indicates an unbeatable enemy and tolls the bell of doom for the builders before they even lay the foundations. In many ways the monuments to the masters of the ancient battlefield where built by those they preyed upon.

Most fascinating about this treatment of the subject was the delving into the Indo-European language. The Hittites were invaders from Europe, which was not at all unusual. There is an area in Anatolia known as Galatia in the Roman world, based on the fact that an army of immigrating Celts [Gauls] settled there in the 200 B.C. The defeat of these Gauls inspired some of the greatest tragic works of Hellenistic art in sculpture.

I do have a problem with the way the producers make the Hittites out to be the only ruthless conquerors in the ancient world. The evidence presented in this documentary indicates that the Hittites were not expansionist by modern standards, rather they seemed technologically innovative on the battlefield, inclined to kill and leave rather than stay and conquer and also obsessed with defensive works at home. The Hittite civil war certainly hastened the fall of the Hittite empire. However, their soldiers served as mercenaries in Egypt in later times, renowned with the sword, and it is unlikely that they died out, but rather reduced their political commitments and moved on. In any case, the empires that relied on the chariot were on the wane and would fall. To this viewer, the big question is what wandering band of barbarians did the

Hittites become when they gave up their experiment with empire.

Did they return to what had originally been a nomadic existence?

https://www.youtube.com/watch?v=QUOKa odz8Bg

In Search of Pre-Human Things

Neanderthals, Denisovans and Pot-Bellied Hill

Below are two video links for Neanderthal curious individuals. I really like the speaker in the first video, who is such a nerd he seems incapable of an agenda—he comes off as the pure fact chaser. The second video is nicely done and helped me understand what the Denisovan question is. At this point it seems clear that scientists are dealing predominantly in answering basic questions and that conjecturing too much is foolish. It is significant that the genetic scientist in the first video uses the terms Neanderthal and Human exclusively for them and us.

One thing does seem certain from the first presentation, that the Middle East was as key in pre-history as it has been throughout history. It seems that there is a small chance that any genes we carry from Neanderthals are left over from before they split off from our family tree. Even if this is the case it does not alter my affinity for them, as I have in common the status of a hunted kind, slated for extinction by a higher [global] power. There is also the fact that at the every place where our kind and their kind met, is the first evidence of monolithic building, long before agriculture, which has been imagined as a pre-condition for monolithic architecture and [I think foolishly] religion as well. View the third video for this.

Whatever the case may be, Europeans and people of European descent managed to overturn every other human society—and even overthrow God—over a mere few hundred years. If we are to look for anything particular about them, the most glaring difference is the conquest of the Neanderthal living space. Whether the resulting advantage over the rest of humanity was due to environmental [not of the social kind, but the actual environment], genetic or learned factors, or all three, who is to say?

Neanderthal and Denisovan Genomes

https://www.youtube.com/watch?v=hoXwQ_H3bRs

Pique Presentation

https://www.youtube.com/watch?v=0R-4OiQVVpc

Pot-Bellied Hill

Gobekli Tepe

https://www.youtube.com/watch?v=eHG9URGDt6s

Danish Girl Charged With Crime

For Not Submitting to Sharia-Sanctioned Rape in Denmark

Beowulf is rolling over in his barrow!

This girl's unlawful use of pepper spray to drive off a man in the process of publicly raping her shall be punished—bitch! Whore! What are you saving it for?

To my readers with families, please begin working on legality-limiting defensive strategies, because this anarcho-tyranny is here to stay, at least until this rotten civilization finally collapses and makes room for something decent and true. Since Europe [Named after a raped goddess, you know!] is further along the socialism/anti-Neanderthal curve than the U.S., it is useful to look to the decadent remnants of the vile West for an inkling as to our near future.

Look, the world has been exploited colonially and now globally. It remains now for the governments that once used our ancestors to screw over the rest of the world to turn their sights on us and screw us over. That's only natural, and the beautiful part is these governments can count on people attacking us with a sense of retributive purpose—they just have to get them here, since blacks kill each other off so quickly they can't expand their population.

http://www.vdare.com/posts/anarcho-tyranny-danish-girl-fights-off-attempted-rape-gets-charged-by-government

'Never Play or Posture at Violence'

A Predictable Outcome by Vox Day

"Did this even make the news? I too wonder what they were trying to accomplish."

http://voxday.blogspot.com/2016/01/a-predictable-outcome.html

-Mescaline Franklin

Tonight I discover that the tactical vehicle my friends saw "prowling" around Baltimore after the blizzard and the absence of my own personal police helicopter over White Avenue was part of an anti-looting operation conducted with federal help, and that a recent, brazen on-camera hitman was apprehended by a Federal task force a few miles from my lair. Last April, when the Mare of Baltimore—in consultation with the DOJ—announced that looting and arson would be permitted city wide, I suspected it was a ploy to justify federalizing of Baltimore City law enforcement, and we are underway, with a 20-agent Federal task force from every branch of federal law enforcement, which is still in town and getting some things done.

Then I find the missive and link above in my in box and begin following a long discussion about some militia types defying the Feds in a wildlife refuge on the upper Left Coast?

This is all new to me and I suppose that readers at this site may well be interested in this brief post and the extensive comment stream. I have no idea what this was about, but if the logic was to garner press attention the people in question failed the demographic media test. In my opinion, giving the enemy what they want, what they need, is never a good idea, and what the Federal Government is ever in need of is an openly defiant target.

Oh, I am glad to report that my personal police chopper is back, having helped apprehend a woman driving a van used to loot pharmacies while the city was clogged with snow.

How Do I Get Published?

Two Neanderthal Resistance Writers Query the Hairy-Backed Prolifidite

"James,

"In looking at many of your books, I notice there is no listing or indication of Amazon publishing. In one (Retrogenesis) you list NERD CHURCH book and list you and another for copyright. Does Amazon not list themselves as publisher? Also: Who retains the rights?"

-David

"Hi James,

"I greatly admire Taboo You, which is my number 1 choice of manhood/barbarian books. I enclose my take on the topic. If you like this, I would be grateful if you could let me know of any publishers worth trying. (I am too broke to do the usual self-publishing.)"

-Regards, Joseph

I use the Amazon subsidiary Print On Demand [POD] service Create Space for all of my print publishing. My web master Charles does all e-books. The kindle template on create Space gets bundled and doesn't get much money back to you. I suggest doing your own PDF and selling it on your own site to finance the site, which is your advertising platform.

The copyright remains mine.

In preparation for my untimely death, I have dispersed my print books into three accounts.

Nerd Church is my agent Erique's account, opened with an email address, which is all you need. Erique and I share that account. He takes the royalties and uses it to buy samples to promote my work for other media like comics. He only has a dozen titles, most of which are duplicated in other books published under my Punch Buggy Books account. I upload the books and purchase from the account wholesale.

Punch Buggy Books is handled by myself and my youngest son, who takes care of the money end while I do the publishing.

DarkEyedGirl books is owned by my beautiful niece, Jamie, who is publishing the second edition of the Sunset Saga, and who publishes anything that I think has a chance of selling or that requires and deserves graphic work.

Copyright is always under your name, even if you go with Random House, unless you are ghost writing or writing a work for hire, like the next Star Wars novel.

Traditional Publishing

I no longer bother to send stuff to Paladin Press because it takes 18 months for them to put it out and I can do it in a day. Likewise, traditional publishing royalties range from 5-15% while Create Space gives me between 20 and 40%. Most authors will not be able to be published by large traditional houses for various reasons economic and cultural at the current time. I am among this group due to the nature of my content.

Dave, you can get published traditionally, but the royalties suck compared to what you can do on your own. Create Space is set up for distribution orders. I can call up my son and say, send Ishmael a copy of this and that, and he does it on his smart phone.

A traditional publisher wants between 3-7 books in the same series, as they don't make money on new authors right off the bat, and will tie you down, typically, to a three book contract, which gets extended every time you fulfill your obligation to give them your next book and they accept.

Traditional Self Publishing

This was once called vanity publishing and is a rip-off on many levels. Do not do this, even if you have the money. Create Space does also offer this service. This costs up to a grand and makes you maybe 50 bucks, and their editors rarely even speak English! Good luck getting corrections done.

Indie Publishing

People like Nine Banded Books, Hopeless Books, Counter-Currents and Mescaline Franklin's Forever Autumn Press [who has published one of my books and will do at least two more] simply use POD providers like Create Space and split the royalties with you.

Create Space

Set up an e-mail account.

Go to Create Space online and sign up.

You will have to fill out tax information so they can pay you and they will report royalties to the IRS.

You will now have your own "Member Dashboard," where there is a button that says "add new title."

Click on that and choose the "Guided" setting. Having done 70+ books, I use the "expert" setting and I'm a tech-tard, who did not learn how to use the Word tool bar until last year and 80% of it is still a mystery to me. If you can read, you are good to go.

To publish a book you need your word file and a PDF generated from that word file.

Pull up the word file so you can have it handy to cut and paste your title, subtitle and dustcover.

After you have copied and pasted your title and subtitle, chosen paperback, and browsed your PDF into the interior section, you will then use their cover creator system, which has you working through 9-12 boxes.

One of these boxes is for your publisher logo, which I leave blank as I can't do graphics and don't have a punch buggy logo.

The entire process is self explanatory. They do have a glitch in the BISAC Code process, which requires you to do it twice in order to get expanded distribution, which are other publisher sites around the world.

You will be given a minimum price, below which you cannot go. If you choose that you will make zero on expanded distribution sales.

David, you put bodies back together and teach in medical school, and Joseph, you have already produced a PDF. If this high school dropout, who can't do long division to save his life, can do it, you can.

The book is your property, and does not get printed until someone buys one. You will basically be able to buy a copy at wholesale for the same margin that is your profit. So, I make $1.94 on When You're Food and can buy myself a copy for that plus shipping and handling. The only reason why I started doing this was because generating manuscripts for my own reference of this same book cost me $25 in toner and paper!

When you buy a book of mine or your own you will know it is a Create Space book when you see the date and place where it was printed on the last page[it is usually a different printer as they have a rotation system that is not regional] making each book truly unique.

I suggest you provide your own cover art as their open domain stuff sucks. You must be certain that whatever image you use is at least 300 DPI or it will be rejected for the cover. Interior images can be less clear, if you wish.

Major publishers do not want to bother with anything that will not sell at least 5,000. Smaller publishers are dying like flies in October. The problem with self publishing is that you have no advertising, and that takes time. Now, a guy like Jack Donovan, who has written a handful of books, basically had to spend five years to sell a four thousand copies of The Way of Men, making scores of online and in-person promotional appearances. I'd rather fight, fuck, write or read, than spend my time doing that. An ugly little lizard like me, who sounds like

Willie Nelson after a huge bong hit, does not bother with such things and contents himself with selling a fraction of what Jack sells.

Whatever you men decide, when you have a book ready to print, I will read it and give an advance review, and help you advertise through our site here. I certainly advise a web site for any author.

So Joseph, the only cost to you to publish a book is you buying it at wholesale.

David, with multiple books ready to publish, you might want to invent a publishing imprint and get a logo going. This makes brick and mortar book orders more likely and is how Create Space is set up, to service small publishers.

Good look guys and I look forward to reading both of your books. When I do, the review will appear in this space.

Oh yes, piss off a Modern Homo Sapien today, please.

'The Sincerest Forms of Life'

Five Minutes with A Fierce Young Mind

James:

I was out with my son at the Harford Mall, thirty miles north of the YoMZ, leaving the parking lot in his luxury sedan, and this professional, black woman was walking in front of him, with her menacing thirty-five-year old drone in tow, glaring this way and that, slowing while we waited, etc. Then he takes trash out of his pocket, holds it out for all of the white motorists waiting for him to see, in this pristine suburban place, and drops it on the asphalt, and struts on. My son was angry. I understand where the adult hoodrat was coming from. He's trying to provoke a confrontation in order to express himself according to his only assigned social value, menace and aggression.

Andrew:

I say, "Do it, trash it up, burn it down!"

I always knew this world was screwed. I cannot wait for Western Civilization to fall. Like those Euros standing back while hundreds of Moslems rape their women. Then this sick system over here is next.

All of the sincerest forms of life have already been eradicated.

I try to do the right thing, support local businesses, give people a chance to do the right thing.

But the right thing doesn't work within a sick system. I get ripped off every time, guaranteed. As a person who sees no sense in procreating in such a toxic environment, I say, "Let it fall."

Western Civilization is predicated on junk, quick cash, easy money, bullshit fiat currency—stuff that does not last, that Styrofoam lawn, houses starting in the mid-three-hundreds that will be shacks in ten years.

Ever since we started burning black stuff we dug out of the earth we've been on borrowed time.

Let it burn.

'Repeat, Repeat, Repeat'

A Mescaline Franklin 'Heads Up Neanderthal!'

© 2016 James LaFond

"Repeat, repeat, repeat… I know this is repetitive, but it is good to see the legal apparatus making the shift, like you predicted."

-Mescaline Franklin

Black Woman Attacks Multiple Elderly White Woman, Gets 20-Years in Jail; After Six Months, Black Judge Grants Shock Probation

http://stuffblackpeopledontlike.blogspot.com/2016/02/black-woman-attacks-multiple-elderly.html

Mescaline, this is what the State wants, unarmed horizontal violence among the subject population, which precludes armed heretical violence against the State, and further justifies armed hierarchical violence against the individual by the State. The author of the linked site, like so many, bought the BS that America was once about freedom and liberty and justice from the beginning, when it was manifestly the opposite.

The first whites moved to this country were disarmed and put at the mercy of Indians, who were armed by the governors and made deals to retrieve/scalp escaped white slaves. Only when the French stirred up the Indians and the white slaves began escaping in droves [1754-63], did the authorities reluctantly arm our forefathers, who were used to throw off the British yoke and kept largely armed up through the Wars of Globalization from 1897-1991. The Global Banker State now has Islamists to keep us in line, so it is time to disarm us once and for all.

As for the criminal in question:

The people with the smallest bone structure in the world are white women.

The people with the heaviest bones in the world—including Polish, Samoan and Norse men—are West African women and their descendents in the U.S.

Although white men are generally stronger and tougher than black men [look at boxing, weight lifting, power lifting, and MMA], white women have no chance against black women as a general rule, so this ideal form of predation will be socially sanctioned. If some white broad shoots this animal or stabs her, she will stand trial.

All is as it should be.

Kneel in prayer and then rise for the liturgy, your mind emptied, yearning to be filled by your masters' thoughts.

'Mencken with a Stick'

Mescaline Franklin On the Perspective Prowl

This is a representative sample of what my young White Nationalist friend from scenic Camden New Jersey sends me a couple times a week. I am thrilled with the last link, which at least puts the extortion partially on the level. The criminal class in America is the new aristocracy. Get used to it. Just like the medieval nobles were front men for the Universal Church, Rayquan and Dooquan [What, you thought I was going to say Tyrone and Jamal, you racists?] are the face of Global Banking.

http://alternative-right.blogspot.com/2016/01/white-privilege-shaming-as-psy-op.html

Andy comes to the same conclusion as "the 21st century Mencken with a stick", I emailed him your 2014 article "I will always be a gringo" where you lay it all out in the last paragraph.

http://www.counter-currents.com/2016/02/the-battle-of-dover/#more-61015

Colin Liddell on the Dover 'riot'.

http://voxday.blogspot.com/2016/02/just-wait.html

This looks like it could be in any American city.

He gets into indentured servants..

http://www.salon.com/2015/12/16/white_guys_are_killing_us_toxic_cowardly_masculinity_our_unhealable_national_illness/

I suspect this is 'clickbait' to get attention but the guy probably believes this shaming a group to make itself defenseless, very feminine.

I don't do anything wrong, can I get an extra nine grand?

-Mescaline

In the Halls of Delusion

A Pang of Judo Angst Echoes in the Man Cave

© 2016 James LaFond

http://supremepatriot.com/2016/02/05/this-college-is-taking-so-called-white-guilt-to-a-whole-new-extreme/#

http://www.campusreform.org/?ID=6873

"I don't think I could ever go back to academia without dispensing a thousand and one brutal judo throws to every single white guilt, offended manchild who sees nothing but wrong in the world."

"Unfortunately, there are laws against that."

"Hope all is well,"

-Adam

Thanks for the heads up, Adam.

There was a time when academia was a place of discourse, debate, the search for variants on the accepted truth and for new concepts as well. That was abnormal.

The proper use of academic institutions is didactic conditioning of servile minds and the encasement of budding souls in tombs of stifling orthodoxy. Awash in more information and possible wisdom than all previous societies combined, we, like the people of Christendom 1,500 years ago, plunge at the speed of female thought into a true dark age, where we belong, ignorant apes scratching our head in the self-imposed gloom of safety and security, the bywords of our age. Life was once lived in a village beyond which most rarely journeyed. In our sedentary age, academia, media and politics constitute the village of the mind.

Not to worry, things area as they should be.

'The Rotting Icing on a Decaying Cake'

[A Case for the Zombie Apocalypse]
Zombie Nation: Day of the Metaphysical
Flesh Eaters by Eirik Bloodaxe

© 2016 James LaFond

Reading from **Zombie Apocalypse Mutant Biker Fighters: The Science, Philosophy, Weaponry and Bullshittery of the Collapse of Civilization and the Rise of Neo-Barbarianism,** page 1-37, by a man who must have a job he wants to keep and therefore has written this hefty 185,000-word tome under a penname.

I promised a reader that I would read his book and let him know what I think, and was quite keen on it, until I opened the file and saw that it was almost 500 pages of small type!

Then I got to reading it, and was very impressed with the almost academic tone and attention to detail, delivered in a brutally humorous style. The footnotes account for half of the content, with the numerous annotations providing a wealth of knowledge.

In this lengthy preface, Eirik Bloodaxe makes a convincing case that we are undergoing an actual zombie apocalypse. He lays out two competing theories, that this is a physical event, or that it is a metaphorical event, with both holding more than enough water to convince this crackpot.

The number of entries on cannibalism—much of it current!—is astonishing, demonstrating a level of research that betokens long hours at the computer. I have already cited Zombie Apocalypse Mutant Biker Fighters in one of my books, and will be using it as a resource, and promise to review each section in its turn. Eirik, I hope you get this thing published. However, if you want a publisher to print it, you should consider breaking it into Two Volumes. This is a big, big book. Congratulations and keep it up.

'If the EBT System Went Down'

A Man Question for the Ghetto Grocer

"What do you think would happen if the EBT system went down, for a week, month, or for good? What would happen to the black community if the welfare system totally collapsed?"

"I say literal mass starvation within a week or two..."

-Guest

Literal and mass, yes.

Starvation?

I don't think so.

Let's break it down, at least in my part of town.

February 2015, robberies of cabbies, sedan drivers and hackers doubled over the previous year

March, 2015, for profit [stolen for resale] looting, during store hours, became common in majority black retail outlets, even when cops were on hand

April, 2015, the Harm City riots and purge, in which the BPD, National Guard, military contractors, and cops from six federal agencies and as many surrounding municipalities, were only able to secure between 1 and 5% of Baltimore City, and left the entire three precincts of Eastern Baltimore County unprotected as gangs of blacks with blunt weapons hospitalized dozens of white men

May, 2015, after the eight largest police department in the U.S.—tasked with securing the 26th largest city [http://www.infoplease.com/ipa/A0763098. html] utterly failed to impose its will on less than 1,000 high school students, and suffered demoralization, Baltimore gang bangers went on a killing spree that sent Baltimore to the top homicide slot in the nation.

February, 2016, carjacking and violence against cabbies, sedan drivers and hackers is on the increase, and resale looting is increasing over last year steadily, having enjoyed a steady rise over the last nine months, due to boldness engendered by last spring's uprising.

I spoke with two current operators of supermarkets today, about the eventuality of EBTs going down, or of another round of martyred-drug-dealer-inspired unrest:

Ben, Clientele 98% Black

"Unless we get lucky enough to become a National Guard staging area or police redoubt, those fuckers will flatten this place. Just this week we had two of them fighting cops on the property—two of them. What about twenty or two hundred? The cops barely handled the two. This is an oasis in the middle of a food desert, nothing but potato chips and booze from here to the Beltway [the I-695 loop]. It 'ill look like a goddamn documentary on army ants. They're not gonna starve, when they know they can overwhelm the cops. If it happens here, you better drop the Navy Seals in to get my fat ass out."

Josh, Clientele 65% Black

[Followed by a spasm of eye-reddening laughter.]

"Christ, Mo, call in an airstrike!

"Seriously, you would have thought it would get better when the EBT drops were finally spread out to the point where we were not on the verge of a riot every month. Remember—fucking Retirement Man—goddamned deserter—that EBT cash hits on day one. Those fat bastards have no cash after the first week. The food drops are spread out all the way to the twenty-fifth, so it should not be as bad as it was—I mean it's easier to schedule staff, but shrink is still up.

"Look, these fuckers are not starving. They aren't even hungry. I have this four-hundred-and-fifty-pound fucker who looks like Haystacks Calhoun in blackface, in here stealing thirty-eight hams—at forty bucks a piece. This guys is wearing silk and Rockports—fucking Richard Roundtree on Similac—and loads up his pickup truck while the hundred-and-twenty pound rent a cop is trying to get through to nine-one-one and Betty is blowing up my cell, while I'm at the bar watching some other piece-of-shit sell somebody else's T-bone steaks to an off duty cop!

"You know the deal, Mo, as soon as the smash and grab crowd knows that the actual starving kids, whose dope addict parents spend all their welfare on drugs, will be getting desperate, they will flatten this place. There won't be a window left on the front end. The registers will be gone—the ATM machine towed away, the stockroom emptied to load stolen trucks, and all eight-hundred-grand in inventory will be sold out of vans and trucks and cars all over West Baltimore for about a hundred-thousand, and eventually some fucking towel-head will open a liquor store here! I just hope it happens during nice weather, so I can go fishing while this shithole burns."

Urban crime is not about poverty, need or hunger, but entitlement, greed and anger.

All of these people make more money than I do just for declining to work, and I'm not looting.

The only real variable is opportunity—can it be done without getting shot or locked up?

What will happen, if EBTs go down, or the grid does down, is that the Police and National Guard will force suburbanites to feed, clothe and house the inner city refugees, emptying home larders at community depots and redistributing the food while the oppressed are assigned quarters in the houses of the privileged.

Bet on it.

Indigenous Survival Grab and Go Menu

Warrior Fieldcraft

Anyone who has viewed movies over the past twenty-five years knows that the preserved Native American knowledge on everything, is better, truer and more functional than anything produced by bankrupt Western Society. The Universal Law of Native American Moral Superiority irks this Neanderthal paleface to no end, especially since feminists have basically hijacked the indigenous independence movement across North America. But, this archive of survival contingencies—even if some can be traced to the hated wasichu or his mongrel children—is a useful resource. The man who operates the Warrior site is one of the hardest working bloggers around, and you wretched paleface warrior wannabes might want to check out his survival archive.

https://warriorpublications.wordpress.com/category/warrior-fieldcraft/

'The Most Generous Nation'

The Death of the Most Generous Nation on Earth

The un-attributed link is at the bottom of the page.

I do not think that Sweden is practicing generosity, but rather abiding its global masters' wish to reconfigure its ethnic mix into something more conducive to the divide and maintain control devices of anarcho-tyranny.

Stop and think, in America, 53% of all murders are committed by blacks, who make up 13% of the population. If that is not a proxy reign of fear, what is? As I write, shootings in outlying areas of Baltimore continue to increase, precisely in this areas to which hoodrats have been transplanted by government agencies, in a direct, calculated, effort to spread violent crime to the suburbs.

Live and let lie, paleface, as you grub for your sodden slice of the pie. Militant Islam needs you, so please, assume this is an accident, and not the framework for your well-considered demise.

https://foreignpolicy.com/2016/02/10/the-death-of-the-most-generous-nation-on-earth-sweden-syria-refugee-europe/?utm_source=Sailthru&utm_medium=email&utm_campaign=New%20Campaign&utm_term=Flashpoints

'A Monster Who is Always Hungry'

A Sorrow in Our Heart: The Life of Tecumseh by Allen W. Eckert

© 2016 James LaFond

1992, Bantam, NY, 862 pages

In this novelized account of the life of Tecumseh of the Shawnee, whose name means Panther-passing-across, Eckert presents the best footnoted historical novel I have read. The amplification notes alone amount to a reference book. Tecumseh is the most Tribal man that this North American continent has yet produced. To save his people and preserve their way of life and the very environment they occupied, he made a life oath, which he kept, to die fighting the whites. He was the fourth in a band of anti-white warrior-fanatics, after his father, his brother and his adopted white brother. His older brother wrote him the following letter—

yes, in English, the Shawnee had been in contact with whites, for 200 years, and knew them well.

In the following letter the modern paleface will, perhaps identify with this stern red man who was called upon by a great white nation to abide by the very laws designed to eliminate him. Note his criticism of the politically correct speech and double-standards of the white elite of his day and compare it to those twisted, yet sacred words, of those elites of our own day. This letter is a treasure that reflects the timeless struggle of free people battling slave societies, a struggle that is always lost, but won't finally end until the last battle.

"When a white man kills an Indian in a fair fight it is called honorable, but when an Indian kills a white man in a fair fight it is called murder. When a white army battles Indians and wins it is called a great victory, but if they lose it is called a massacre and bigger armies are raised. If the Indian flees before the advance of such armies, when he tries to return he finds the white men are living where he lived. If he tries to fight off such armies, he is killed and the land is taken away. When an Indian is killed, it is a great loss which leaves a gap in our people and a sorrow in our heart; when a white is killed, three our four others step up to take his place and there is no end to it. The white man seeks to conquer nature, to bend it to his will and to use it wastefully until it is all gone and then he simply moves on, leaving the waste behind him and looking for new places to take. The whole white race is a monster who is always hungry and what he eats is land."

-Chicksika, elder brother of Tecumseh, to Tecumseh, March 19, 1779

Chicksika and Tecumseh both died fighting their sworn enemies in the teeth of the execution of George Washington's successful policy of killing all wild life and felling all forests—the precursor of the campaign to wipe out the buffalo, which occurred on a large scale in Kentucky—that would lead to the defeat of the trans-Mississippi tribes. Ironically, these men, who were so much more masculine then their enemies that it was as if two different species contended for

North America, once slain, left behind the lesser, quitting, half of their people, with the result that American Indian resistance leaders are now committed feminists, who cannot even tolerate the white veneration of the warriors of their racial past.

That is victory as a wasteland, as predicted. Ironically, the cause of freedom and tribal autonomy for which Tecumseh died for is continually attacked by modern mixed-race Native Americans who have bought only the material artifice of their past and stand rank and file among the white monsters of the State to which they eagerly enslave themselves. It occurred to me some time ago, that when the bodies of the great Indians were killed, their spirit did not live on in their bloodline, but in the haunted minds of those who fought them on their own terms in service to something they revered less then their enemies.

A Sorrow in Our Heart is the story of all tribes who have been crushed by the machinery of civilization, is brilliantly done, and should be read by any tribal reconstitution leader or masculinity advocate.

Primate on Primate Crime

And the Violence Guy is on the Case!

"Jim, could you analyze the monkey's technique and poise? On one hand, the monkey is holding the knife in an icepick grip, an indicator of murderous intent. On the other hand, he does not seem to be very committed."

-B

Okay, B, I am glad, that for once I get a serious inquiry from one of my readers.

A. If we look closely at the second video window, and note the Mohawk haircut, we see that he was on the warpath, and became hyper-hostile once imbibing some of the Whiteman's fire water.

B. The fact that he chased men away from innocent women marks him as chivalrous.

C. The grip, while indicative of pursuit and hyper-aggression in the hands of one of us oversized primates, in his case, appears to be a kingly pose, as in the picture of Arthur Pendragon taking the sword from the stone.

D. The fact that, when the reprobates he chased off called in uniformed reinforcements, that he then abides by the Castle Doctrine and takes to the roof of the keep in defense of his women folk, is the fourth part of this chain of events, definitively linking this monkey to the still restive soul of Arthur Pendragon. Had the enemy kept the film running up until the point where he leaped from the battlement screaming, "Excalibur," we would know for sure. As for whose fault this is:

E. 1. That was the Whitemans' fire water.

F. 2. Arthur Pendragon was white, with his tarnsmigrant soul presumably remaining white-identified.

G. 3. The Welsh lake skank who gave Arthur the blade was white.

H. 4. And he stood one against many as paleface warriors are habitually prone to do...

All evidence mark this as a racial crime against innocent Brazilian colored folks. It is Whitey's fault, plain and simple.

Also check out the Israeli News article link at the bottom, which was a well done piece of humor.

https://www.youtube.com/watch?v=mfKGWAivpkA

https://www.youtube.com/watch?v=kBrPftyNxTM

http://www.israelnationalnews.com/News/News.aspx/208290#.Vsi7Tvl95D8

'The High Country of the Soul'

Wild at Heart: Discovering the Secret of A Man's Soul by John Eldredge

2010, Thomas Nelson, Nashville, 1-19 of 256 pages

Do you realize how unusual it is for a fighter to be able to keep an appointment?

Most men who have the psychology to fight do not also have the discipline to keep commitments and also take their combat game to higher levels. Not long ago I agreed to meet a young man at a certain hour and place, two weeks out, and intentionally did not check back in with him. I wanted to know if "he was the guy" that I could leave my combat material and experience with. There are local men who have long worked with me who have already taken their portion of our joint efforts. But Baltimore is fallow grown—worked clean of potential fighting men years ago. If my local successors are going to be able to do better than waste away on their own masculine island, they will need an outside connection, a Brother Band, outside of this corrupt place. I was confident he would show up, and he did, to do me a big favor.

The man has what he wants in terms of family and occupation and is still probing in my insane direction, so I know these other aspects of his masculine nature are in sync with his sense of adventure. It is not as if he is single, and will throw his masculinity out the window upon marriage, as most men do.

The next phase of the test was to challenge him to a type of fight that only a handful of men in the world can be gotten to do—the type of fight that all real men used to do, a well-considered duel with blunt weapons, not a death match, but a test, a test most so-called men in our society decline.

I posted the challenge online—a rude act— and he called me minutes later, a dark tone in his voice, accepting the challenge, which, in reality, is a passing of a brutal torch, a torch I think he is fit to carry.

It is of great interest to me that this young man sought me out based—ultimately—on a reading of John Eldredge's book for Christian men, Wild at Heart, which he gave me as a gift, and asked for my opinion on.

John, in this book—which I suspect that former Satanist and extreme right wing masculinity advocate, Jack Donovan, used in formulating his four point masculinity code—seeks to rectify Christianity and masculinity, which, as he admits, is no easy task, but this reader believes, is a necessary one if we, as humans, are going to survive the monsters we have created in our fits of godlike aspiration.

Before I go any further, I think my pagan, heathen, Nordic, agnostic and even atheistic readers should try this book—if you are of a mind that the masculine heart of Man is worth rescuing. I have read the first half of the book and reread the first chapter, deciding that it is one of those volumes too important to encapsulate in the type of review I now reserve for comic books and novels. Ideally, a concurrent reading of The Way of Men, Wild at Heart and The Philosophy of Freidrich Nietzsche, by Mencken would, I think, zero in on the crux question of masculinity in our context, as we are sucked into an ever expanding, collective, feminist, secularity.

Where Donovan presents the aspects of the manly man in four dimensions, in the context of enemies without and an ambivalent female presence within, Eldredge concentrates not on the qualitative and quantifiable aspects of the man, but on his experiential yearnings, making the two volumes very compatible. Where Jack speaks of "strength, courage, mastery and honor," John speaks of "a battle to fight, a beauty to rescue and an adventure to live."

John's evocation of scripture [old Jewish patriarchal stuff, for you heathens] and gospel [the good news that God, in the form of a heretically heroic Jew, died for your heathen sins] is mixed with his life experiences and communicated largely through reference to popular movies. He spices this with quotes gleaned from a deep reading list. This book was written to reach the widest possible audience of Christian American men, and to use the sacred and secular media influences in their life experience to light a spark in their "masculine heart," or fan the spark that is there into a flame.

Not only have I found Wild at Heart useful, having not completed it, but it has encouraged me to read the Scriptures for a seventh time. Most importantly, I see John Eldredge's effort as a bridge that might possibly enable a masculine alliance between Christian men who are inclined to resist the feminine secularization of life, and the various pagans, heathens, deists, agnostics and assorted masculine-oriented individuals and groups that are rejecting the very same system that strikes horror into the masculine Christian heart.

I encourage all of my readers, of all ages, to read Wild at Heart.

Thank you, Sean.

Oh, young man, in the shallows of this coming spring, when on the dueling ground, if you notice that pot-bellied old heathen drifting left—beware, that's the leg he can still lunge off of.

'He's Not a Hero'

The Strange Talent of Luther Strude by Justin Jordan, Trado Moore and Felipe Sobriero

2013, Image Comics

I recall, as a boy, reading comic books, and seeing ads featuring strong men selling anti-bullying training regimens, with graphics including a big guy kicking sand in the poor geek's face. I decided, at age 11, that the answer to such treatment was to not red comic books but become the bad guy in the comic book! The Strange Talent of Luther Strude is seemingly built on exactly that impulse.

The aspect most endearing about the comic is the Hercules advertisements and the scenes of Luther training like a monk in his room while his twerp friend encourages the tall, geekish—but possessed of an Elric like structure—Luther to do banal staff like macking babes. But no, Luther just wants to kill with his hands, to be a singular lethality. There is not a tiny hinny in this dark high school comic. Luther is—essentially, I think—one of the Columbine boys, with muscle instead of a trench coat and gun, avenging himself on a sick world.

If you are a comic book reader that has stepped away from the genre due to Thor with a clit, the conversion of white heroes to black, the overall leftward tilt of the ethos, and the increase in gay superheroes, try The Strange Talent of Luther Strude, in which the option to become a monster is preferable to being what the sick, sissy world wants you to be.

I'd like to thank Erique for this review copy.

'My African Research Assistant'

Women, Science and Politics in a Harm City Medical Lab

A woman recently told me of her experience sitting with a group of fellow, white, university-educated women, discussing the upcoming election of the next emasculated criminal and chief of this bloated trading-post of a nation and a candidate that they reviled above all. The other women were scientists who worked in a medical lab.

"I had to sit and listen to these women talk about what a terrible person Donald Trump is. I kept my opinion to myself, until the one woman began speaking of her African research assistant. She said,

'My African research assistant actually suggested that if Trump were elected he might be able to straighten the country out if he ran it like a business.'

"I was very interested in this turn of conversation, as I have friends who are African—decent, educated, classy people with traditional family values—not what we have here in the U.S. with our willfully stupid, violent African Americans.

The other woman said, 'I hope you straightened her out,' and the first woman began describing how she spoke in ebonics, like an African American hip hop personality, to her assistant, even calling her 'girlfriend.' It was shockingly disgusting to see this level of ignorance from a scientist. African Americans prey on Africans, hate them, share none of their values. To talk down to this woman like this was disgusting. So I said, 'You may want to consider that Africans have entirely different viewpoints and values than African Americans, that they do not share the same culture.'

"They looked at me with a kind of dreadful astonishment. The next order of business was to begin discussing why this Trump person—who I know nothing about—was so terrible. This largely focused on him being evil for having money, which is an understandable prejudice, and is why I don't trust any of these politicians, because they are all wealthy beyond my conception. What shocked me, and is something I will never forget hearing, was the key reason on which these women agreed that Trump was a ruinous presidential candidate. These two college-educated white women were most troubled by the fact that, and I quote, 'He's so white.'

"I recently stopped working in Baltimore because—ever since the riots—every second African American would look at me with a belligerent, palpable hatred in their eyes, and my black coworkers would harass me for the crime of being a white woman. And these stuffy suburbanites, working in their lab and living in their elite white community, think that we need more of that, that we should live in a gangster rap nation, with all of the attendant criminal values and base, violent morality?"

-Melody B.

Sharing with Simone

One Minute on the Bus Stop with a 45-Year-Old Pale Face Breeder

© 2016 James LaFond

Simone was waiting for the #15 at Frankford and Belair at 3:30 in the afternoon, headed out to work the evening shift as deli clerk at the local supermarket. The armed bank guard was pacing to her rear as she waited for the bus on the corner and she felt pretty safe, what with it being light and with many people about of all descriptions. She is normally very vigilant about letting any black youths around her. But the bus was coming and she was getting ready to board and checking her fare, and "smash," she was clothes lined by a teenage forearm across her glasses, knocking them off, and knocking her to the ground. The hitter and an accomplice took her wallet, [as she was careful not to carry a purse, being aware of her prey status], her cell phone, and her bus pass.

She was able to stagger home on her own, as no one offered to help her, including the armed guard. Once home she was able to call work on her roommate's cell phone, resulting in her losing her job for missing the shift.

This is one of the most dangerous corners in Northeast Baltimore. For ten years I walked past this spot almost every night of the week. It was bad then, in the 1980s. Now it is a murder hub, and warm weather is coming, main got polar bear season in the ghetto.

See the deluded links below.

https://foursquare.com/v/frankford—belair/4e6e7474483bf10521844b3d

https://www.walkscore.com/score/belair-rd-and-frankford-ave-baltimore-md-21206

'Three-On-One'

Biking Around Lake Montebello

"A few years ago I was biking around the lake. It was before the improvements, wasn't as many people there as you find now. I was biking for my conditioning. I can no longer bike around town because of my hearing. I wouldn't last long on the street. You have to be able to hear the traffic.

"So, I'm doing about twenty-five in the bike lane and there are these three yos walking towards me in the bike lane. The one raises his fist to punch me and a hit the brake, which is a very hairy thing to do at that speed with a bike. I managed to maintain control, stopped, and then turned. They were about thirty feet past me. I figured three-on-one was a fair fight and motioned for them to bring it. But they kept going in the other direction."

-S.J.

http://www.bing.com/search?q=lake+monet bello&form=CPDTDF&pc=CPDTDF&src=IE-SearchBox

'These Oregano Traffickers!'

Jack's Official Marijuana Legalization Article By Jack Perry

First, I would like to note that in Baltimore, oregano constitutes half of the pot you buy from black dudes, and garlic powder like 20% of the coke and "heron." I like Jack's point on this issue, but would suggest that a totalitarian government will never let its subjects have unsupervised access to thought-affecting substances. Our thoughts are supposed to belong to them. In my un-drugged mind, for I have never fathomed why people want to mess with their brain chemistry, the litmus tests of a State, as pro-human or anti-human, are:

1. Does the State tax the subjects? If so, they are evil.

2. Does the state restrict access to mind-enhancing, or altering agents? If so, evil again.

3. Does the State reserve the right to use lethal force? If so, even more evil.

4. Does the State force its subjects to use force on others. If so, all the more evil.

5. If the State answers yes to all of the above it is 100% malevolent, a force for the extinguishment of humanity.

Thanks, Ishmael, for keeping me current on Jack's work.

https://www.lewrockwell.com/2016/02/jack-perry/feds-wage-civil-war-people/

Pale Faces for Sale!

Liberalism and White Guilt: a Man Question from Ronald

"I just got done beating the heavy bag, these clowns had me so pissed. What do you think, James?"

-Ronald

There is a link to a bunch of whites playing slave and begging black forgiveness at the bottom of the page, which really burned my friend, Ronald up.

Okay, Ronald. I respect you as a fellow boxer, and really do value our relationship, but—honestly—I'm insulted.

Bro, do you really expect me to buy any of this chattel?

I scrolled through 24 frames of guilty wannabe white slaves, and did not find a single attractive wench or strong man. Now, you can make it up to me by going to North Korea—I heard they have a short sale on raven-haired shorties, and getting me a matched pair for football season. Oh, yes, and a strong Tang Soo Do man for a bodyguard—I'm not what I used to be you know...

Oh wait, let me check again—there might be a worthy bed-warmer cavorting with the dyke husband of the first African American president...

Yes, indeed, tenth row down [below the gray scroll panel], far right. I will take the young blonde on the far left, who Hilary seems to be ogling for her own uses. I' don't need a discount—and will take an express delivery—winter is almost over you know!

Thanks, Ronald.

Seriously, Ronald, I hurt myself laughing. I want to see a pageant, an auction, a pre-sale spelling bee to see if any of these narrowassed wimps would qualify as a research assistant or proofreader!

Maneuvering against the All-Weather Hoodrat?

A Hero's Welcome Heads Up from Samuel

"Hi James,

"The crack of the bat, the ceremonial rolling of the drunks, it's that time of year again."

-Samuel

http://www.washingtontimes.com/news/2016/feb/25/michael-schroeder-is-second-marine-attacked-and-le/

Thank you, Samuel, for posting yourself as a scout for this stuff. I really am dependent on my readers for news. Local news I get from coworkers and my roommate's copy of the Sun paper. Other than that I'm on Planet Graphomania. In the 1990s I was a daily

Washington Times reader. This is the paper for which Fred Reed used to cover crime.

It is notable that the police always deny that any violent crime is ever part of a larger pattern, even when occurring on the same night with the same attack pattern.

Many times have I heard palefaces say of the North American Hoodrat that preys upon them that cold weather is proof against the hoodrat. However, recall that the North American Hoodrat, while exhibiting some characteristics of its African ancestors, have evolved in close proximity to the Norway Rat which is rampant in the ghettos of the Eastern United States, and at home in arctic environs. The Hoodrat is acting out in order to gain respect from the enemies of its political masters. Survival minded palefaces should be careful not to assume that their opponents in what has been an openly declared war will not adapt.

It astonishes me to know end, that when militant people declare war openly, the targets and designated enemies continue to assume they are at peace. This is as insane as denying that the U.S. Government has been waging war against citizens since 1974, when the president declared an internal domestic war which has been vociferously reaffirmed by every one of his successors across party lines and is vigorously prosecuted by tens of thousands of law enforcers—utilizing military equipment—annually.

To prevent such attacks on city streets:

1. Walk in the street, against traffic.

2. Walk against walls when on the sidewalk.

3. Turn your head 90 degrees on every step.

4. Actively seek the enemy with your eyes and ears.

5. When changing directions, make sure no one is within three paces.

6. Do not pass doorways, alleys, etc, but cross the street diagonally, from a point before, to a point after the dark opening.

7. Cross the street often, and diagonally, opening your field of vision.

8. Pick up a brick, stone, board, bottle or chunk of curb or asphalt.

Julian Fights Back!

Ten Minutes with a Tough Middle River Broad with Pink Lipstick and Joan Jet Hair

The entire time that the woman is speaking, in her blue paisley scrubs, the author is stocking the cottage cheese and nodding, occasionally managing to get in a word.

"You see that guy, that big long-haired guy, he's off. I know it. I work in the medical field—a respiratory therapist. After working in enough hospitals you get a vibe for the crazies.

"Out in Los Angeles, I went to the Beverly Hills pizzeria for lunch and this black guy tried to take my purse and keys while I was waiting for the pizza. I fought him, fought my ass off, back-and-fourth. He finally got my purse, but not my keys. It made the news.

He threw my purse in someone's yard. I punished his punk-ass.

"When I was working down at Hopkins, headed to my car on the parking lot, this big black guy was walking in front of me, looking at me diagonally over his shoulder—real shifty like. I just knew something was up. Then when I got to my car he came back at me. I opened the car door a crack and when he got close slammed it on his ass. He went flying back and looked up, saw the police helicopter circling, and ran. They got him, were already looking for him when he came for me. He had just beaten and raped another white woman on the street in broad daylight. Not me!

"I hate junkies. Out at the Baltimore Coffee and Tea Company, the junkies all come down from the methadone clinic. They were all loud, so this eighty-one year-old lady asked them to keep it down and these junky bitches started giving her shit. No dice, I got up in between, confronted the ring leader, a pregnant, stoned whore with a baby in a carriage, and said, 'Bitch, I will fuck your world up.' Oh yeah, you bet that loser stepped off.

"I grew up in Mount Washington—all Orthodox Jews now. Now, I guess I have the Middle River accent.

"Last week I was at the Wawa [farm store] and I noticed this white guy sneaking up behind me—in the store. I'm at the counter and here he comes creeping up, backing off when I look, then creeping up again, measuring me for the purse snatch. Fuck that! I turned around and said 'Punk, I will fight you to the death. You better step the fuck off!'

I slung my purse over my back and put up my dukes and said, 'Bring it, pussy willow!'

"And you know what he does? He scoots around behind the soda display and changes his clothes. I was holding my phone up over the shelf filming that shit, saying, 'Came with an escape plan too, didn't you, you junky piece-of-shit!'

"And off he went. And on top of all of that shit, white junkies messing with you, and big black guys attacking—the black bitches are taking our men. Back in the day they always used to complain about white bitches taking their men, now their taking ours. Doesn't leave a white girl much to chew on you know—do you work here all the time? Are you new? You seem like a nice man. I'm sick to death of crazies, punks and junkies. A girl wants a real man, some strong arms, you know!"

"See you around, baby!"

A Page in a Book against Time

Counter-Currents Posts Iron and Paint by James LaFond

Books against Time is the motto of Counter-Currents, which is the webzine that reaches deepest into the literature of the past from the right of our cultural spectrum. I owe my introduction to Evola, Spengler and Bowden to the work Greg, the editor, has done toward the end of preserving the best thoughts of our keenest minds.

Since Ann suggested I submit something to Greg a half year ago, I've been hoping I would come up with a nonfiction piece that would make Greg's grade.

If you have not read it, I wrote Iron and Paint in an hour and a half on Saturday the 27th of February, after spending all night at work mulling over the impression that had saddled itself upon my mind back on Wednesday, when Mescaline Franklin took me with him to photograph a piece of Western history slated for the all-devouring dustbin of ignorance.

I e-mailed it to Greg and he got back to me within an hour, having decided to run it on Monday and asking for a photo from Mescaline, which is featured in the article.

If you have not read Iron and Paint, or would like to see the photo, click on the link below.

One thing I should have added, about the horses, is their attitude, which jumps out at me in the photo. Jackson's horse is impatient for battle, and Lee's mount hangs its head somberly, its rider cursed to survive the end of his Age, unlike the hero at his side.

http://www.counter-currents.com/2016/02/iron-and-paint/

Iron and Paint

The Lee-Jackson Memorial: A Rational Interpretation

© 2016 James LaFond

There has been much anger expressed on either side of the racial divide in Baltimore, concerning the so-called "Lee-Jackson Memorial." This past week, on a fog-shrouded, drizzling, winter Wednesday, a young White Nationalist from out of state came to Baltimore on his personal mission to photograph Caucasian monuments before they are taken down by the New Left. I accompanied him.

Before continuing, if your parents avoided damaging your brain in childhood, you may wish to access A Dictionary of Symbols by J.E. Cirlot.

If your mother was drunk while you abided in her womb, just grab Transformations of Myth Through Time by Joseph Campbell.

If Mom was a stoner and Dad was smacking her around before you were ejected from her womb to eat lead paint, view an NFL game, and understand that you will not have access to the prime vagina dancing on the sidelines, because you are not one of the Homeric bruisers on the gridiron, nor one of their puppet masters...

Monumental architecture and the subordinate statuary are generally limited to erection in un-free social circumstances, with the minority representing the fleeting victory of some un-free soul [such as an athlete or hero] in the face of Time's yawning maw, and the majority representing messages to the slaves of the future by the masters of the past, in support of the masters that have assumed their ancient powers over the minds of the masses and the bodies of all.

One must be careful not to isolate individual works of art that comprise larger municipal monuments, as these entire parks are often integrated metaphoric schemes, which were conceived in the context of a general education that no longer exists. When Wyman Park was built it was known by most U.S. denizens that, though the Union prevailed in the Civil War, the Confederacy fielded better fighting men at all levels. At this time, circa 1910, Union and Confederate veterans of major battles were sometimes gathering to honor each other. These healings and the known history of the Civil War, generated something of a demon question:

"How could the Confederacy, formed as a rebellious entity for the very purpose of **extending** the reach of forced human servitude, in one of its crueler forms, into the unconquered West and Latin America, have produced the most courageous, competent, heroic and honorable combatants?"

At Wyman Park, in what was essentially a border state, the architects of this park seem to have made an attempt to put this demon to rest within the larger context of a monument honoring the Maryland men who fought for the "preservation of the Union," on land, river and sea.

Below I shall do my best to describe the Union war memorial that is Wyman Park.

Facing Charles Street, which is the most culturally significant primary street in Baltimore, is a jutting eminence of stone, backed by a marble half-circle bench. This viewer took the bench as both an invitation to sit and ponder the monument, once viewed, but also as a symbol of deliberation, the seats now unoccupied by the men who passed sentence on a former age and who no longer walk among us.

On the pedestal is a single union soldier, representing the anonymous men who did most of the dying, for the cause—as stipulated by the epigram—of preserving the Union.

The soldier stands above the Anvil of Victory, indicating a long, arduous struggle.

On either side are army and naval symbols.

On the soldier's left stands Pallas Athena, goddess of thoughtful, civic, war making, of the just striving of the collective "demos," marking this monument as inspired by the battle dead monuments raised by the ancient Athenians [from which our democratic principles descend down through the ages]. The shield of Athena—for the goddess was generally seen as the protector of communities in ancient statuary, contrary to the drivel of postmodern "masculinity" advocates—is emblazoned with the naval and army symbols.

On the soldier's right is Nike, winged goddess of victory.

The soldier has divine sanction to left and to right.

Below the statues, on the flanks of the eminence, are carvings of sailors to one side and soldiers to the other, striving heroically, under great threat, in a collective, suffering, but undeterred, body.

On the eve of the age of mass, nationalistic warfare, no more fitting message for the individual fighting man could be left in the name of his heroic predecessors.

Behind the monument stands a children's playground, offering the civic lesson—perhaps an apocryphal or spurious one, as I am not familiar with the date of its inclusion—that in the wake of the suffering of men, children might safely play.

A wooded hillside gives way to an artificially deepened valley, evoking the Valley of the Shadow of Death that is War, congruent with the Christian imagery subtly worked into the victory monument above.

A stair rises from the valley—which is representative of the Civil War that divided the nation—into a stand of trees. These trees manage to evoke the forest when the viewer stands beneath the next monument. The forest is the key context for heroic striving across a vast body of Western Mythology, a metaphor with particular resonance in the United States as "the superseded past," for this land was the most heavily forested in the world upon its settlement, and at the time of the monument was almost completely deforested. [Forest cover a hundred years ago in the Eastern U.S. was a much less than today, as agricultural production has since been moved primarily beyond the Mississippi.]

Amid this "forest," [often symbolizing the hero's quest] on the far side of the park, on a platform that sits lower than the "plateau" upon which the main monument is placed, is a flat marble platform on a low ziggurat-style tier. On this platform, is an eminence that grows awesome as the viewer walks beneath it, as the two men are seated on horses, twice human scale like the soldier and goddesses of the main monument. The horses represent—by default, throughout Western history—the servitude of not only these beasts, but of lesser men as well.

The men are "Stonewall" Jackson, hero general of the Confederacy—though no word about the Confederacy, or the "lost cause" is mentioned. Jackson, as he did in his storied career, wore a simple soldier's cap, not the general's hat of his commander, Lee, who sits next to him. It was well known to every student of the Civil War that Lee claimed that he lost the key battle of the war at Gettysburg, for lack of Jackson, who was his "right arm," and Jackson does sit his horse to Lee's right.

Lee is cloaked as if against the rain, or the night, or in mourning of the pending loss of the man he depended on so often for victory. The scene is stipulated in the epigram as depicting the parting of Lee and Jackson for the last time, as they ride off to supervise their brilliant victory at Chancellorsville, at the close of which Jackson will be killed, accidentally, by his own men. For the Southern cause, this is the moment of ultimate victory and of unavoidable doom, all in one.

The feeling, in ancient Hellenic terms—which was the pattern of the Park—is of the archaic, heroic period, the time of kings and heroes, before the rise of democratic communities like Athens, when monumental architecture is of single heroes, who will be incorporated in later collective monuments, like the Parthenon.

There is a laudatory quote by Lee, about Jackson, on his side of the monument, which I do not recall.

There is a quote by Jackson, that he would follow Lee "blindly," under any circumstances.

The statue of Robert E. Lee, cast in black iron like the rest of the figures, is grave, as he sits on Traveler, his storied horse. Jackson, Lee and the entire Army of Northern Virginia constituted one of the most successful battlefield fraternities in masculine history. The men revered Lee like a father—and more, loved him—sometimes refusing to fight until he was safely in the rear, and then driving in a suicidal fury at the enemy, often in bare feet. Indeed, Lee got caught out of position at Gettysburg trying to get to a shoe factory so his men would have something to wear on their feet in the coming winter.

This monument cannot be understood without the above knowledge of the devotion of these men to each other, the only devotion described on this image of iron and stone.

Most ominously, as Lee and Jackson look into a parking lot, over ground seemingly intended to represent the past—of some lost age—the man who Jackson has said he will follow blindly anywhere, has taken his binoculars out of their case, but does not look through them.

The monument of a divided nation that is Wyman Park, will lose its lesson, and its soul, when a people blinded by hate remove this tragic portion of it, and in so doing remove their own past without knowing what it was.

Post Script

On the saddle of Jackson's horse, a stick, crudely placed and painted the color of iron, holds a pair of wooden shackles, meant to indicate that Jackson represented slavery. This adulterous addition to the Union Monument, dedicated to the Soldiers of Maryland, is streaked as the paint fades under the elements, in sharp contrast to the unmarred iron it was intended to amend.

When one looks across the street to the left, a view of student housing for John's Hopkins University looks like an old English debtors' prison, with bars and iron grates barricading the ground floor windows and doors, the left most building defaced with numerous no trespassing and security notices.

As one looks across Charles Street, in a southeasterly direction, past the barricaded dormitory and the emergency call station, an ancient church looms, ominous and holy, except for the armed guard patrolling the front. The viewer has the sense of standing in a deeply divided nation, where—according to all appearances—the acts of learning and worship seem to be undertaken in the utmost peril, as a twenty-year-old woman looks this way and that, like some furtive, hunted creature, at midday, as she descends the stairs of her ancient lodging with a basket of laundry.

Jackson would have surely detailed some lucky, barefoot soldier to carry that basket past whatever danger haunted her so.

Find a link to the location below:

http://www.bing.com/images/search?q=wyman+park&qpvt=wyman+park&qpvt=wyman+park&FORM=IGRE

'To the Gothic Playground'

Nero the Pict on Harm City History

"My God....That piece you did on Wyman Park and its Civil War statuary was amazing. You know the next time Mr. Franklin makes his way south you might suggest a visit to Loudon Cemetery. Don't know if you have ever been there. It is the final resting place for a whole mess of dead rebels. The juxtaposition with the surrounding area is quite striking. I foresee a time when the Confederate wing will have the markers knocked down and a statue of Oprah dropping a squat erected in their place.

"Also, he might appreciate a visit to the gothic playground that is Greenmount Cemetery. John Wilkes Boothe is interred there, 'Sic Semper Tyranis' and all that.

"Take care man,"

-Nero the Pict

Mister Franklin, has already done a photo study of the forgotten monuments to the anonymous fallen of the First World War and is dedicating the next couple years to amassing a photo archive of Western memorials that seem likely to be erased. We will try and team up for as many of these as possible.

Thanks for the kind words echoing down from the sodden ground above Yo Adrian's Invisible Wall.

'A Lawyer Living on the Ghetto Edge'

Our Ever-Helpful Guest Introduces the Z-Man

Off topic, The Z Blog added you to his blogroll!

Maybe return the favor and add him to your links...

http://thezman.com/wordpress/

He is a lawyer living on the ghetto edge

I always read Z and LaFond in tandem...

Updated daily, he posts gems like:

"Post-modernism is when a people forget all of the lessons of previous generations and start painfully re-learning them."

"The people running things employ persuasive morons to sell their position to the persuadable morons. Arguing through a megaphone leaves only one option. The side that is the loudest wins. It's why Progressives will work free of charge for a turn at the megaphone. "

"Laws limiting free association were intended to eliminate the organic structures that naturally oppose authoritarianism. It's why the Founders made freedom of association the first item in the Bill of Rights. It's why Progressives have been making war on it for close to a century."

"My chief complaint against libertarianism is that it is a convenient hiding place for people unwilling to take on the Left. If you reject central planning of the national economy, but are afraid to be called bad things by the local lunatics. In the culture war, libertarians will never go over the top and will, once in a while, turn their weapons on their comrades. You just can't trust them to fight."

"Gun control has always been a proxy-debate that is more signalling than a debate. Good whites from Yankeedom see guns as a stand in for southerners in particular, but all bad whites in general. After these shootings, the good whites get to have their day for acts of public piety. It's why they say the same things over and over. Rituals are like that."

Maybe fix Eradic to Eradica while you're at it.

And another blog that linked to you several times, and where i initially found out about LaFond, with a big F, is:

http://www.isegoria.net/

Both sites would be worthy additions to the links

I have no affiliations with them, I am just a fan...

'Why Don't You Simply Move Out of Harm's Way?'

A Man Question from Our Guest

"Pardon me, but why don't you simply move out of harm's way?

"And shouldn't you talk junior out of buying a house in Baltimore County, that's no place to anchor. I don't want to be rude but I just don't get it, as you said you have enough writing and hood source material already. Isn't buying a house here like driving a car off the lot?

"You are asking for it by staying...

"Is it the battered wife syndrome?

"Escape while you are still in one piece, you could also make more money in some small town teaching self defense classes.

"Or if you want to stay in the supermarket business, German discount retailers Lidl and Aldi are currently massively expanding in the US and are both looking for staff!

"Just Lidl alone plans to open hundreds of stores in 2018, 2000 even by 2020, they will need thousands of new people, especially the first stores opening in the Greater Washington, D.C. area would appreciate you specific urban skill set.

http://www.lidl.com/

http://aldiuscareers.com/opportunities/

"Lidl and Aldi are top dogs in Germany, even your great Walmart couldn't compete with them, they closed up shop in 2006 in Germany, they also withdrew from South Korea the same year, Walmart that is.

"And no wonder, Oreos taste like crap compared to even cheap German store brands, it's not even close."

My Progeny

Okay, my youngest son first.

His older brother is stuck in a house he cannot afford in Harford County—the place everybody fleeing Baltimore moved to between 30-15 years ago. I was just out there and saw three hood rats walking with skateboards, not riding, but carrying skateboards as weapons.

Glenn knew, on his own, that following the rest of the Baltimore rabbits was not bright. Indeed, today, I saw twice as many for sale signs in the bedroom community my mother, sister and oldest son have all moved to. My Millionaire Uncle has moved from Harford County as well—to Florida—because they are bussing in hoodrats out of Baltimore, nullifying the property values of the houses people bought and the security they bought them for, and the safe retirement my mother fled Baltimore for. Now she looks out her door and sees hoodrats, one year before her last mortgage payment!

Glenn works in the D.C area, around Alexandria Virginia, and since he is just starting his finance firm gig he can only afford a 250K house.

To get into a hoodrat-free subdivision around the nation's capitol costs 500K and up. Low income areas around D.C. are just as bad as Baltimore, and is why half of South Baltimore residents work in D.C., because living there on a slim budget is bad news.

To move to Pennsylvania, would be a two hour drive one way. He wanted an hour and a half commute, tops. He's at an hour and a quarter instead of an hour because I talked him out of moving into Baltimore City, where all of his young coworkers are congregating. Of over 200 locations he looked at, he is in the safest. I will devote an article to this later. The guy that is really screwed is his older brother, with two kids, plummeting resale value under his hard-working ass and rising crime. Two cops got murdered around the corner from his house last month. The guy had been sleeping in a parking lot you can see from my mother's house.

Understand, Harford County was the Promised Land for white flight—a trap. The county is fighting the State of Maryland, the Feds and the City, to keep them from shoving their crime down their collective throat, but to little avail.

Glenn has every intention of becoming a CEO and owning a mansion and a Tesla in rural Maryland, PA or Virginia far away from hoodrats. But for now, living in rentals he can afford 12 miles past the city line is far more dangerous—and more expensive—then buying a much nicer place in the safest area of Baltimore County. It is a quirk of the anarcho-tyranny strategy used by the State, that pockets of safe suburban municipalities escape almost unscathed while others are ghettoized. This will be the subject of the upcoming article Hoodrat Homesteading.

My Excuses

As for making a living teaching self-defense, I'm currently being booked for about $50 per week in Baltimore. I coach real combat, which is nigh unmarketable even for those with marketing skill, which my reptilian personality does not have. I am currently one of three coaches who have moved from failed schools into a combat arts refugee camp. Money is in women's fitness and children's programs, neither of which I do.

The grocery business?

Aldi runs a good chain, placing locations in ghettoized areas to catch overflow Walmart business, primarily. The lack of concern for their predominantly female low-earning staff, left handling money alone with only one other female employee typically in the building, is criminal.

Yes, I once managed a supermarket and was quite good. I could get a six figure job and live in a safe suburb, but would work in a ghetto—guaranteed they would put me where my qualifications scream to be applied, working in the ghetto. So what would have changed for me?

I would go from living in the ghetto on foot in torn up clothes, to working 70 hours a week in the ghetto in a shirt and tie, and getting my windshield replaced every time I fired some ex-convict for fucking a cashier in the lunchroom.

There is also the little matter of my writing. In order to work in management—which is where the only living wages that permit vehicles and modest home-buying are in the retail food business—I would have to reduce my output from a book a week to a page. In four years as a manager I managed only three articles.

What is more, I would have to take down 80% of my articles from this site and most of my non-fiction books, never to write another ghetto grocer or Harm City article again. In writing fiction, if I ever wrote a black gang banger character saying the word he says most often, and an employee or supervisor got a hold of the book, I would be let go.

I consciously burned my bridges the way I abruptly resigned from my management job in order to make room for a writing retirement. I did this largely because I felt myself slipping mentally, and knew, that if I somehow outlived my father and grandfathers, that it would not be as a sharp writer, but as a reader, wondering if I might have been able to be a writer had I not wasted my life feeding welfare recipients.

But, these are just excuses.

After I resigned my management job, I turned down nine other opportunities, some of which would have had me in a nice location—my entire life lived outside of this rats nest.

I could say, and it would be true, that the government has slated every place where elected officials and campaign contributors do not congregate in gated communities for ghetoization, and that I am staying in a zone that is headed down that road ahead of Maybury Fuck You For Free and am documenting the fall of Western Civilization from the front lines, which I am doing. This is the kind of shit I tell Mom, true, but not the reason for my living on $600 a month in the most violent city in America. I do make about 10K a year working my 20 hour job and writing. I donate the coaching money to the school, pay 1K per hear for the crime of not signing up for free health insurance and give money to my family. I just gave my son 10% of my annual gross to pay his moving expenses, since I'm no longer strong enough to haul his furniture.

My Reason

What is the real reason I live in a crime-ridden metro area?

From March 20, 1963 through July 5, 2010, I was a meat-puppet, a grinding gear in the corrupt body economic that is our sick society, in which 999 out of 1,000 people who think they are human are not, but are rather bio-economic units powering the machine that eats the souls of the one-in-a-thousand true humans. Living such a life, I dreamed and read—enjoying a life of sorts within my own mind—until, at a certain point, I feared for my sanity, as the things I had read, and witnessed, and figured out—would not leave my head!

From July, 5 2010 through the late summer of 2015 I actually lived as an ascendant human being, searching for the truth, hoping to touch God's pinkie with my pathetic brain, training, writing, fighting, snarling at gangs of punks that other pale faces live in perpetual fear of—I lived, and was lucky for that.

Since my physical prowess left me like a winter breeze on one late summer morning, in a mere moment, I have counted myself among the undead, the lucky portion that can at least recall living as a human instead of a subhuman cog in a puss-lubricated machine. What is left of me is, in essence, a faltering archive trying to upload itself before its hard-drive crashes for good.

I moved to Baltimore in 1981, one step ahead of an attempted murder charge, with the intention of making enough money to fund a suicidal one-way trip to South America with the goal of randomly murdering drug traffickers with a knife until being shot to death. I was side-tracked by a woman who had a sick son, and who ended up giving me another, so felt honor bound to live long enough to see them on their way.

My dear Guest, if I did not write, did not have sons to avoid shaming, I would paint a masterpiece of violence, and go down in history as a mass murderer with few equals.

As things are, I am content to fade away while I write.

On Racial Lines

Big Jake: Stateside in 1966

I'm seventy-one. When I went to Nam in Sixty-six there was plenty of tension between the races. After basic training, I went to gunnery school, scored high enough to be an instructor, and became a door gunner on a Chinook, one of those flying buses. I boxed, and had some swagger about me, but was not stupid—like my no-account cousin who talked me into takin' our leave in the white town off base—turning left comin' off base rather than turning right.

I was a big young man—heavyweight—but I weren't no fool, even at that young age. I knew if somethin' went down I would be all alone, so I slipped a razor under my cuff, somethin' up the sleeve if necessary. There we go, turning left commin' off base, the sentry shaking his head. We were not even onto the road headed to town, but coming to it, when this big car pulled up.

Out steps a white boy, as big as me.

I figure I can handle that without goin' up the sleeve.

My cousin is runnin' his fool mouth.

Out step another white boy, as big as the first, so I start to go up my sleeve, this fool still runnin' his mouth, "so en so" and "this and that."

Out of the back seat step a boy so big I had to look up at him—and things began to crystallize with some clarity in my mind, namely that I am standing between a no account fool and three big boys. So I gave his trifling ass 'the look,' and he shut his mouth.

Then, the car tilts, and the biggest white boy that has ever been birthed on God's green earth rises up, towering over the rest. I nodded respectfully, as they stood there with arms crossed, let that razor stay where it was, and walked off down our side of the road.

They did not follow, simply drew a line, and I can't say as I'd blame them. Hell, I didn't even like my cousin!

That's just the way it was, lines and whether or not to cross them. Now there are no lines and your own folks will do you in quicker than you can say mashed potatoes. There are things to prefer about now, just as there are things to prefer about then—just not the same things.

Change, brother, it comes for us all.

'Is There Intelligent Life on Earth?'

Ostara Publications

I was currently loaned A Brief History of the Warr with the Indians in New England by Increase Mather. Such primary source material is incredibly valuable to an investigation into our history, obscured as it has been by the jingoistic lies and revisionist misfocusing of actual events and conditions as practiced by the sham academia cult put in place in the late 19th century in the United States.

The publisher which has reprinted Mather's candidly brutal record of his own people's sins, and more importantly of a fanatically pure view of life that modern Americans refuse to believe informs their own evolution into what they have become, has a number of offerings in the open domain area that have been made available via the create space template.

Check them out at the link below.

http://ostarapublications.com/

'Crucifying Picts'

A Glimpse of The Plight of a Pennsylvania Paleface

This past Tuesday, on a nice, balmy, winter afternoon, I was driving to dinner with a lady friend when we saw that three pig wagons had a car pulled over. We ended up stopped at the light at Northern and Harford and I rolled down my window to listen, ten feet from the bust site.

I was immediately reminded of Robert E. Howard's story Worms of the Earth, in which a Pictish barbarian is crucified by local Roman officials, bringing down the wrath of the Pictish King, Bran Mak Morn.

Well, Nero the Pict, up there on the other side of Yo Adrian's Invisible Wall, they got one of your Pennsylvania boys, who committed the crime of driving into a mixed-race Baltimore neighborhood with PA license plates. I know one PA construction worker who spent 40 days in the Baltimore City jail over a simple traffic violation.

The 30-year-old bearded, paleface was handcuffed on the curb as drug deals occurred across the street between blacks in front of the nail solon, where a friend of mine once told me the smell of pot bricks stored there for distribution was so strong it burned his eyes!

Hoodrats are prowling around in twos, carrying skateboards, not riding them.

Two traditional drug set lookouts on bicycles are circling the scene.

Maybe this was their "connect," a medium-sized fish, the mule for The Man.

The only paleface civilian on the street is cuffed, his wallet and I.D. open and scattered on the curb as he talks to the skinny drug task force cop who has a 50K pickup truck that looks like it belongs on an NFL commercial.

The other, stocky, white drug task force cop is standing over the Pict [he is pale and tattooed and from up north] and speaks with the regular black patrol cop about the latest piece of tactical equipment. This task force cop has a black escalade. [These are vehicles confiscated after drug arrests.]

The lead pig is asking pointed and leading questions over and over again to the guy on the curb, who is explaining over and over again that he drove to Baltimore to visit a friend. His car is a low-end five-year-old sedan.

The pig wasn't having it.

My lady friend is angry over the fact that thugs—who openly hunt us on the street, who stop heading toward her when they hear the locks on her car door click, who all of a sudden turn away from me when I stop and look at them—are consistently ignored by cops while white guys are arrested three times more often in this neighborhood.

I tried to explain to her that any arrest, leading to a conviction or not, that is written up as a drug bust, even if this guy just has a joint or pain pill on him and is released the next day, goes towards the next federal drug war grant, so is a priority. There are no federal grants for protecting citizens from criminals spawned by this very same drug war.

The spiral must continue.

One note for people on prescription medication:

If you take one or two dosses of medicine to work in your pocket or purse, and get pulled over for any minor reason, you may very well be arrested for having undocumented drugs on you. I have seen it happen many times. Unfortunately, this means you have to carry your prescription bottle with your address and name on it, which means if you get mugged they now know where you live and have information to assist in identity theft. Also, if your coworkers know you are on medication they can steal your entire prescription, which has become very common in supermarkets.

'A Legacy'

Colin Flaherty Profiles a Fallen American Hero

None has done a better job of profiling the fall of Western Society via social media. This is a sobering montage of the inane self-deification that is currently the centerpiece of emasculated American culture, as well as the focus and repository of the scientific ambitions of Asimov, Clarke, Pohl, Heinlein…

Author Colin Flaherty Tells Story Of Black MN Thugs Shot By White Victim! Was This Racist?

https://www.youtube.com/watch?v=hBS4E TSPGdQ

Beyond Evilzon

Reading LaFond Digitally Beyond the Reach of Empire

© 2016 James LaFond

"How come you don't also sell these books in your own book store? I'd rather get the digital version pdf here, and even pay more for it, rather than having to deal with evilzon. Knowing all $$$ goes goes to you would be a bonus on top!

"Or does the Amazon CreateSpace Independent Publishing Platform demand exclusivity?"

This is how you do it.

Make a donation in the amount you think the book is worth to you via our donation link. Then e-mail me at jameslafond.com@gmail.com, and say, hey James, that donation I just sent you was for Stillbirth of a Nation and I will e-mail you a copy, the very same copy I used to typeset the Evilzon version. This is a perfectly good adobe pdf, just like anyone with Word 2007 could make on their computer. It, however, would never cut the mustard with my webmaster, who only places for sale e-books that meet his aesthetic criterion. And, since he has been busy doing the Harm City Safari guide for this past year, we have stopped offering e-books. Charles has made no bones about the fact that my PDFs are ugly! Hideous!

So, be warned, the PDF is going to be as lacking in graphic quality as the print book!

There is also that matter that I produce a book every week or two, and that—with Charles' other commitments—it takes him a month or two to make it into a PDF that meets his stringent standards, which means our e-store will not catch up until I buy the dirt-bath farm!

Actually, the Create Space slaves of Evilzon demand very little, seem to have been quite cowed by their ominous master, and are very responsive to my requests for help, on those rare occasions when I am actually aware that I am screwing up!

Thanks, Our Honored Guest, once again for a helpfully pointed question.

For those who are wondering, our donation button is on the right column of the main page, in the form of King Nero the Pict, seated upon his plastic throne, holding the cardboard crest of his house, which seems to be an ongoing request for financial and military aid from Rome against the savage Gaelic reavers commanded by Cormac Mac Art...

With a Big F

Our Xenophobic Guest Discusses Who is Committing 90% of Violent Crime

Fun fact Mr. LaFond: 90% Nonwhite Violent Crime Rate FBI

http://newobserveronline.com/90-nonwhite-violent-crime-rate-fbi/

"Nonwhites commit at least 90 percent of all violent crimes in America, and the least white cities are the most dangerous, an analysis of the latest Federal Bureau of Investigations (FBI) crime statistics has revealed."

That's why "xenophobe" is such a funny insult; A phobia is of course an irrational fear of something that poses no actual danger. It's like pest control asking if you have arachnophobia, when calling to report finding a million spiders crawling around your home...

Xenophobe would also make for a great book title!

Or "White Xenophobe"

by James LaFond

with a big F

Harken to LaFond Respond

Actually, although xenophobia has come to denote irrational fear in our own twisted English-language society the word was borrowed from the Greek, and means precisely "Stranger-Fear." The Lidell and Scott Greek English Lexicon is a great resource for tracking the corrupt devolution of our sissy society, just by tracking the corruption of words we borrow, that change meaning to support political agendas.

Now, since almost all crime is committed against us by people we do not know, namely strangers, being a xenophobe is to be most rational. The biggest lie in law enforcement is the constant mantra that most violent crime is committed by people who are known to the defender, which points up the fact that the only crimes our society is much concerned about is spousal abuse and acquaintance rape.

Why is virtually all aggression committed by non-whites, when whites are the largest segment of the population?

That is simple:

Imagine a herd of sheep, the shepherd, the sheep dogs and the wolves [these last being the reasons for the shepherd and the sheepdogs in the minds of the sheep, which all Judeo-Christian folk—and our current brand of atheism is very Judeo-Christian in tone—are conditioned to regard themselves as, helpless, domesticated animals in need of a shepherd.]

The majority are the sheep, who commit no violence. The three minorities—with both of the canine breeds serving the purpose of keeping the flock together where it can be easily managed by the shepherd—commit all of the violence.

The value of the sheep to the shepherd is in the fleece, not killing the sheep, but shearing them. We might equate this to taxation. A lamb, ewe or ram that is afraid of the wolves and the dogs is more handily driven to the shearing—which I think occurs on April 11 for most of us.

From 1700 through 1950, the black American was a docile breed of person, more unlikely to commit violence than any whites other than Quakers and Amish, and much less aggressive than those nasty Native Americans. In fact, although blacks sat on their hands and waited for whites to free them from bondage, we are currently seeing Civil War scholarship and movie making focused on the few black Union soldiers who were victorious, in an obvious attempt to convince blacks that they have always been militant. There is incontrovertible evidence that most black slaves never fought their slave masters, never even tried to escape.

When interracial violence did erupt in the post slavery period the blacks always got the short end of it, the whites ever proving more aggressive, more effective in the use of force. After Jack Johnson beat Jim Jeffries a handful of whites were killed to dozens of blacks.

From 1900 through about 1960, there was more interracial white on black crime than black on white, and the police in urban centers made a policy of randomly attacking blacks for no reason. Whites—stupidly— used to say to this, that this was in order to keep the black from attacking whites, which proved to be the opposite. For as soon at police violence against blacks spiked in the early 1960s, black violence against whites skyrocketed, and continues to climb.

This sick nation systematically brutalized a formerly docile laboring population, in order to turn them from sheep to wolves, at the same time discouraging whites privately, at every turn, with news casts and visits from Officer Friendly in elementary schools, to not take the law into your own hands. Who of late middle age today, does not recall the constant drumbeat of news and TV crime drama declaring the impropriety if 'taking the law into your own hands?" This is the same generation that fled urban centers in droves throughout the 1970s, 80s and 90s. People of my generation were brain washed into the absolute belief that we did not have the right or even the responsibility, to defend ourselves, that the police would do it. All the while the police where attacking and warping the minds of the new feral race, the Thug Tribe of Hip Hop America.

Now, where once tough Polish, Greek and Italian guys used to beat up blacks for venturing to find menial employment in their Baltimore neighborhood, and blacks would suffer raids from police in their neighborhood just to "set a tone" we now have the opposite, a docile white population terrorized by blacks and able-bodied white males of the lower classes constantly harassed by police for no reasonable cause.

What is amazing to me is how far palefaces have fallen. That the race who hunted the proud warrior peoples of this land to extinction now allow themselves to be preyed upon by such sissy black men, who lack the spine even to stand up to their own women, is a wretched state of being. Nine out of ten hip hop thug adults could not beat a tough twelve year old of the old school in a fight, and these wimps manage to rule these streets, largely with their bare hands and shoes, rarely even using guns? How pathetic!

I hope the Latinos come in and wipe out the lot of hoodrat and labrat masses. As I write MS-13 is beginning a machete terror campaign in East Baltimore, hopefully one day to turn these weapons on the degenerate palefaces and feral blacks of Baltimore, and cleanse the land of weaklings who so yearn to be sheered by their shepherd in return for the dubious honor of being relieved of the burden of defending themselves and their loved ones.

Paleface Enemy #1

The Pigs: The First in a Series of Poor Character Sketches of Paleface Foes to the Neanderthal Cause

The following is for entertainment purposes only and in no way represents the views of the author, who is a well known keyboard comedian.

Raphael is a friend of mine of more than twenty years, a man who is a brother to me. He is half-Norse and half-Spanish, a unique Neanderthal cross-breed. He lives in a small home in East Baltimore. His car has been broken into twice. On one occasion he saw the thieves. These are two innocent, unarmed, youth of the Hip Hop kind, one white one black, the Paul McCartney and Steevie Wonder of their era.

The Hip Hop youth is the frontline trooper in the State campaign to exterminate palefaces.

For decades of writing on this subject I have resisted the notion that palefaces are slated for extinction. But, with mounting evidence every year, I have finally crumbled before the most rational conclusion, that the means towards the actual end rather than the falsely stated end are the measure of the State's intent.

It is an unfortunate fact that more palefaces are trying to wipe out palefaces than the hip hop slave thugs of the liberal autarchy. So this series of articles will profile palefaces that are out to get palefaces, both on principal and for gain.

In this case, Raphael has tried to be a good citizen, and has called and spoken with the BCPD many times. Since the pigs have declined to act against the thieves, Raphael threatened the thieves. This brought the police to his door, with a statement, that if anything happens to either one of these doomed hoodrats that they are coming for him. Raphael is almost sixty?

These thugs will likely be offed by one of their own kind some day.

What do the pigs do?

Do they defend him or his property, fulfilling the 'protect and serve' motto on their car?

No.

Do they defend the criminal and his activity?

Yes.

Pigs only have one thing—for they certainly do not have the support of their traitorous masters—and that one thing is the power to use force with a reasonable assumption of getting away with it. That force, if used against the other agent of the State's attack against palefaces—namely Hip Hop hoodrats—no longer comes with a reasonable expectation of getting away with it. However, no one cares when a paleface is gunned down by cops, which happened two weeks ago in Eastern Baltimore County to very little fanfare.

So, how do we palefaces deal with pigs?

Never speak your mind to a pig.

Never speak your heart to a pig.

Never speak the truth to a pig, unless the truth clearly exonerates you.

Lie to pigs whenever you think it serves you.

You must get used to lying to the enemy, for they are creatures of the Lie, are ruled by the liars that master them, and by the hoodrat liars that manipulate them.

Do not extend honor to a dishonorable enemy who holds all of the advantages except for those superior thoughts that are within your mind.

The pig does not have a mind of its own, but is rather, a kind of meat-puppet—and he oh so painfully is aware of this, knows well the strands of power from which he dangles— easily manipulated by thugs and politicians alike.

Do everything you can to stay off of pig radar, which includes calling them. Recently a woman was raped and applied for a gun permit after her rapist was exonerated due to mishandling of her rape kit. She is being denied a permit because the pigs know she has a valid reason to use it and they are, above all, jealous of the only thing they have, power to use force within politically correct limits.

If you report breaking and entering in your area, and the cops talk to you, and then the drug addict doing the breaking and entering gets capped by his drug dealer for being behind on payments, the pigs come for you.

Lie to the pigs.

Be a stranger to the pigs.

Minimal information is the rule when dealing with pigs.

Only answer questions directly and to the point.

Never give a reason or a feeling.

Play dumb as much as possible.

They like to think they are smart and are not, so playing stupid usually works.

Never forget, that the pigs are the enemy, and, like any overconfident enemy, can be tricked into acting on your behalf, so long as you are not honest and open with them.

Do not make the mistake that the Indians once made, of being honest with a dishonorable enemy, or your kind will one day dwindle as has theirs, to the verge of extinction.

Many a great Indian chief from Metacomet, to Crazy Horse, to Sitting Bull and Geronimo, where done in, not by palefaces, but by fellow Red men in paleface employ. When you see that paleface cop, realize that he now fights for global forces as far beyond his understanding as were the industrial concerns that ultimately paid the salaries and bounties of the Indian police and scouts were beyond their understanding. In their ignorance the Red men did in the best of their own kind for the honor of being the slave of an enemy, losing even more than did those they betrayed, for they lost themselves as well as their world, where those they betrayed at least went to their death as a human that they recognized, not as some leashed parody of the enemy. Do not underestimate the magnetic slave instincts of the petty palefaces that would rule you at a traffic stop, at the gas station, at the farm store—when he cuts in front of you and does not even pay—and at your own front door when he comes after you for defending it.

'What Do You Think of Libertarianism?'

A Man Question from Rob

"James, what do you think of Libertarianism, its pros and cons, for the masculine man who desires liberty?"

-Robert H.

Lets' start with two pros and two cons:

Pros

Libertarians understand economics better than any other politically identified group, most of whom know less than nothing about the generation and transfer of wealth. Primarily, libertarian arguments are useful in talking sense into the more intelligent liberals.

Libertarians, unlike liberals and conservatives, understand that the State, or Government is its own entity, a living social organism that quickly grows more powerful than whatever political faction that seems to be in control of it. For instance, very few right-wingers realize, that by electing a strong leader to battle enemies overseas, that the result will be a stronger government, that, when it reverts cyclically to the control of left-wingers, will be that much more potent as an instrument of domestic oppression.

Conversely, the left-wingers fail to realize that when they employ government agencies to oversee private affairs at home, that those powers will inevitably by hijacked by predatory business interests and used to undermine the economic position of the common man.

Cons

Libertarians generally believe in and abide by the non-aggression principal, which renders the philosophy itself impotent in the cause of implementing its own principals.

Libertarians generally seem to believe that the 'Founding Fathers' of the U.S, were libertarians, when the majority of them were either bankers with monopolistic designs or slave masters seeking to wring more profit from their chattel. The actual libertarians of the Revolutionary Era were those escaped and released white slaves who headed into the Ohio Country to escape the plantation economy and the natives they battled against.

And, for the tie breaker, it goes to the cons. Libertarianism is a purely materialistic view of life, which appeals predominantly to atheists. Atheists, however, tend to be drawn to collective worship of the human cause, to save and extend every life at all costs, and generally abhor libertarians. What is more, libertarianism ultimately comes to a point of agreement with the left, regarding the body as more important than the mind, the material world more sacred than the transcendent. For instance, in his otherwise very good audio article, The Truth About

Slavery, Stefan Molyneux, the foremost libertarian spokesperson today, declared that escaping from or fighting against enslavement made no sense to American blacks during the plantation era, as they were assured better shelter and food in chains than on the run! The problem with all materialistic philosophies and ideologies is that they lead to such sell-out conclusions, a chief taking glass beads to disinherit his grandchildren, a slave dying in chains rather than in combat, a tribe giving up its identity for t-shirts, a nation throwing away its ideals for the cause of obesity.

Lastly, libertarian views may only be understood by the rational human mind. So, when competing with sentimental conservatism and collective liberalism, with the identity-based right and security-based left, a libertarian view can only hope to appeal to the tiny minority of intelligent people. Public education and the media have essential disabled the vast majority of Americans from comprehending views more complex than a snack-food commercial.

'Less Dramatically Arch-Neanderthal'

Altrugenics Analysis by Koanicurgus and other Physiognomy Experts Determines that LaFond is Paleface Neanderthal Survivor!

Okay guys, thanks, this blew my archaic mind. The site is fascinating and since I'm no Bram Stoker, but rather a Bran Mak Morn, I will have to take your word for it. The greatest compliment was the conclusion that Robert E. Howard was "Less dramatically Arch-Neanderthal than LaFond!"

Here I might quote Cory Bracken about Big Water Blood Song, my first novel:

"The best thing ever written by a Neanderthal."

But, Cory would be wrong, for, according to these men, the best thing ever written by a Neanderthal would be Worms of the Earth by Robert E. Howard, a story of our bloody-handed ancestors.

May you crush the enemy, see them driven before you, and lay with their women where you may.

http://www.altrugenics.com/forum1/viewtopic.php?f=35&t=540&p=5790&hilit=lafond#p5790

Hauling 'Human Garbage'

World's Strongest Man Vows Rough Justice and is Fined

© 2016 James LaFond

"Saw this article and thought of you. More of the same really, but I this one seems more blatant than usual."

"Stay safe out there,"

-Dylan

http://www.dailymail.co.uk/news/article-3442481/Next-time-ll-hit-baseball-bat-Former-World-s-Strongest-Man-vows-rough-justice-human-garbage-migrants-fined-40-000-refugees-hiding-Britain-bound-lorry.html

Thanks, Dylan.

This past weekend I had a discussion with a friend about the fact that police have told him that he will be arrested and charged if he hurts the people breaking into his car. It is about time that the myth of property rights died. Another friend recently showed me a text by a British friend of his who described how blatant burglars are in Britain and that the police will arrest you for hurting burglars. Now this news that a trucking company boss is fined for threatening stowaways—France deserves to fall.

Please, in whatever area of the civilized world you live, realize, that you will likely be prosecuted for harming any criminal who attempts to take, damage or use your property.

Faces of a Dying Nation

Sissy Terrorism in Frogland

"The fact they now they can risk this shows what they think of the French. Sheep."

-Mescaline Franklin

Africans in France terrify French Women with replica Guns to expose "Racism"

You know, Mescaline, if I stabbed this guy I'd go to prison. But, if he tried this in Baltimore he would probably get shot by a distant cousin long before he got around to getting shanked by a Neanderthal.

https://www.youtube.com/watch?v=4Du2M_8JHuU#t=30

Glory Season: 2016

The Fresh Face of Racial Predation

On Wednesday, March 9 summer came to Harm City. By Thursday the temperature was at 80 degrees and hot pants, tube tops were barely covering girls and aspiring Mandingo cast members were walking around shirtless, flexing their unemployment like an honor.

Under the starlit Wednesday night sky, I headed down off the ridge to Northern Parkway at 9:03 p.m. I heard police sirens, as I had heard them all day as "Africa rose up in the blood" of melanin-rich Harm Citizens.

Not all of the locals were such hoodrats. The porch of the house where I catch the bus was a meeting place for two brothers and a friend—of about 16—as they were dropped off from working their after school jobs. They discussed their video games for a while and went on their separate ways, courteous, and not thuggish in the least, three Baltimore City black youth, who decline to take the bus, working class kids not taking the working class option, where they did this time last year.

While I am at the stop two cop cars from Northern Parkway turn up toward the ridge, screaming up the side streets toward a place where the police chopper is headed to and other sirens can be heard converging on. After three minutes the chopper is making a tight circle, about a quarter mile east of my home at Walther and White. Then the ambulance siren sounds and the chopper pulls off.

When the bus pulls up it is packed with the former number of passengers before last year's April Purge.

Might things be back to normal, I think?

No.

There is one terrified Chinese guy, one super-fit, grungy paleface and the normal load of adults returning from work, and the security guard headed to the night shift at the hospital—another Neanderthal. The entire back deck of the bus is packed with a mob of upper middleclass black kids with $400 in phone and $500 in attire each, waxing boisterous, trying to sound ghetto, and failing. These boys are 13-15, and are headed across town to the Purge territory on an adventure. They are going on a 15 twerp raid. These twerps do not offload until the bus is safely back out in the county. These are not city boys, but upscale punks who all loaded at the head of the line at Towson Town Center. They off load, with two of them attempting to stare menacingly at me as they strut and flash hand signs and hoot like animals.

The bus was then nearly deserted for an uneventful ride, except for Old Man Mike spilling vodka down the aisle as he boarded in a sloshed condition and the driver advised, "Yo, brutha, you leakin'. Watch my coach."

Once offloaded at Stemmers and Old Eastern, the other passengers huddled under the shelters for a transfer as one girl, who had been in phone communication with her ride, hoped hurriedly into the waiting car.

I like walking a hunting ground at night. It is invigorating, particularly on a breezy summer night in winter. As I walk through the park I can hear the train's call out over the ditch it rumbles through a mile to the west, and can hear northbound Canada geese overhead. As I hit the tiny Middle River Park I see the homeless insane lady is back with her bags and blankets, mumbling inaudibly as she stares blankly ahead from the painted iron park bench. As I cross the bridge the three foot egret, a wary friend for five years now, looking verily archaic, keeps one eye on me as he fishes in the muddy shallows at low tide.

Seemingly a life time later, I am back on the #55 bus on Northern Parkway, headed in the other direction, pretending to sleep behind my sunglasses—which protect these old eyes from the rising sun—as the digital bus clock reads 8:13. Three, non-ghetto speaking, well-dressed, middleclass, ebon saints are standing over me, about two to three feet off, discussing in hushed tones the possibility and advisability of "Getting' Santa Claus when he hop off."

One answers, "Hop, shit, he got a cane."

The third says, "Check, see if it a pointy cane. He might stick us."

The heavyset black girl next to me on the side bench seat facing the back door is glancing at me nervously, as if worried that she is going to see something bad happen.

"What you think, Yo?" whispers the second to the first.

I then turned the head of my aluminum and steel umbrella cane—a gift from Mescaline Franklin—brought it to check, and stood straight up, to which they all three drew back from the hips up as the first speaker, the tall boy, whispered, "Pointy."

To that I tapped him on the shoulder and headed to the front to offload there, as a fine, lithe looking wench of perhaps 22, with rich mahogany skin and a long disdainfully drawn face, reclined there against the guide bars polishing her leopard skin-painted fingernails.

Sun glasses have more than one use.

As I walked home, up to the ridge line where sits the old plantation house in which I rent a room, I wondered at the fact that these two groups of boys looking for trouble where under 16, not city residents, using a county-to-county line that only dips into the city for three miles, are obviously middleclass— probably the sons of government employees—and seemingly vey new to thugdom.

To me, the three real city hoodlums that threatened me late last year at Harford and Bayonne, and the four who tried to run me down on a nighted city street at the end of last summer, were simply practicing the oldest form of economics. But these privileged youths, going on expeditions to find old palefaces to attack—these are racists, produced by a system designed toward that ultimately sanguine end.

This is their glory season; their time to emulate their heroes who defeated a city police force in open battle on internationally broadcast video. These are the tepid princes of a new thug ethos, who, when they do attack, will have the full backing of The Media State.

Dispossession

A Guide for the Predatory Globalist

© 2016 James LaFond

As I have spent the past decades researching the crooked birth of our tilted nation, a pattern for the dispossession of native peoples has emerged. And, for all of you Native Americans—being those people born in the United States of America—this wealth of documented experience has, rather than being used to educate the leaders of the future, which is suddenly upon us, has been suppressed to the extent that unveiling it now will do you little good. However, for you globalists, you predators of domesticated humanity, whose stewardship over the Meat Chute of Souls has earned you your place in as yet to be written history, the following are those eleven keys to your success. You might wish to codify these for the benefit of future macro-parasitic generations.

Suppose you discover a land full of people. What now is a globalist to do?

1. Disease is a good start, those born in Africa seemingly ideal for weakening native populations. The more disease you can introduce to the native population the better. For this reason open borders are very important.

2. Charity is the best first step of the globalist. Send your most wretched subjects—ideally those least useful to your purposes in their own native land—to the foreign shores and trust to the charitable impulse of the natives to take them in and feed, clothe, house and educate them as the English settlers of Virginia and New England were cared for by the natives of that age, who passed on their own agricultural and survival methods.

3. Drugs and their introduction into the native culture, such as the English introduction of rum to the Indians and opium to the Chinese, are ideal for rendering the native social order weak and unstable.

4. Purchase their land while they buy your drugs, giving your transplanted folk a rallying point and a morale boost, so that when war breaks out they will fight with the fervor of the native born.

5. Breeding is a must. Emulate the English in New England, who each fathered 10 to 12 low-quality, neglected children to the 2 loved and educated children of their native enemy. Sure, we like to think quality matters, but there is nothing like 6-to-1 odds to embolden your folk and see you through military setbacks.

6. Moral Sanction, ideally based on an introduced religiosity which is at odds with the native beliefs, will put in place a social friction that can be used as a tinderbox for righteous expansion. Toward this end, you must first gain local converts from among the natives to your own collective beliefs. The establishment of schools is key to this end. In light of step 10 [see below] it is preferable that you introduce a dualistic [black-versus-white, good-versus-evil] worldview. Anything more nuanced may fail to produce your ultimate end, which is managed discord.

7. Submission of the natives to your beliefs and cultural norms may begin with drafting agreements for separate but equal treatment, but has quite another goal.

8. Integration of people unequal before the law is the final pre-purge phase. For instance, if you can force mixed living, schooling and judicial circumstances, in which either people are given special treatment or privilege, it shall serve your end. In the worst case scenario, accepting that your people have less rights, will eventually serve to establish a guilt complex among the natives and permit a see-saw ethos in which they will eventually cede privilege willingly to your now embittered folk. Absent this type of weak-minded native, it is preferable that you go in with the aim of establishing privilege for your transplanted folk. It worked well enough for the Normans in England and the Spanish in Mexico at the point of a sword, and worked without initial force for the fanatic English Puritans. Therefore, a puritan model is recommended for sowing discord.

9. Separate Language within a forcibly integrated macro-community will favor your cause, which is civil war. Once you have peoples speaking different languages and adhering to opposing worldviews, forced to live in the same space, war will eventually erupt.

10. Media Control must be achieved, either through the earlier education initiative or, as the Spanish and English did, erasing and supplanting native forms of communication through outright vandalism, suppression, or economic incentives. Europeans forms of recording ideas were cheaper and quicker and enabled them to bury enemy information as they propagated their own view. The formation of a morally superior body of ideas, and the suppression and vilification of a morally inferior worldview, will eventually insure a radical orthodoxy among slavish folk that will bolster your cause via constant pressure against dissident public expression.

11. Extermination must be the end goal once war is joined, which is why disease is such an important initial ingredient, and why the

ennui caused by the introduction of drugs into a transformative cultural matrix is so important. Drug addiction is the surest method for suppressing childbirth rates among advanced cultures [Japanese and European], and of ensuring the orphaning, mistreatment and retardation of the children born to less sophisticated but fecund peoples, [such as African Americans]. Management of the dispossession endgame will therefore focus on targeting those natives experiencing depressed birthrates as they try to adjust to economic scarcity, while utilizing the anger inherent in those peoples who have suffered severe cultural erosion but have maintained their population, placing micro-generation after micro-generation of physically abused, emotionally disturbed and spiritually empty youth under your influence. In this way, just as the Europeans who took America used "praying Indians," Indian scouts and Indian police to defeat Indian patriots, your descendents will be in a position to set the lower orders cultivated through economic dispossession, cultural erosion and drug addiction upon the dwindling native enemy.

Huzzah!

Review

1. Disease

2. Charity

3. Drugs

4. Purchase

5. Breeding

6. Moral Sanction

7. Submission

8. Integration

9. Separate Language

10. Media Control

11. Extermination

'Your Opinion on Slapjacks/Saps?'

A Man Question on Handy Survival Weapons

© 2016 James LaFond

"Also, do you have anything self defense related on your keys?

"Is something like a Kubotan, ever worth the trouble?

https://upload.wikimedia.org/wikipedia/commons/d/d0/Ku2.JPG

https://en.wikipedia.org/wiki/Kubotan

"A silver one should be indistinguishable from keys on security tape. Your honor, all he had were his keys, or umbrella..."

-Guest

Okay Guest, the Kubotan is something I have used. I recommend the plain cylinder or the plain cylinder with glass-breaking tip, keeping in mind that cops who find you with it will add it to their collection, as will court house officials, federal building security and airport personnel. So buy a few. Do not buy or carry the version with the two spikes protruding between your knuckles. These will be classified as brass knuckles, and may carry stiffer penalties in some municipalities than an oversized knife.

Keys themselves are an overrated weapon. You are better off using your fingers in a cupped cone and raking the enemy eye with your fingernails than trying to stab at a face with hand held keys.

Saps, blackjacks, slapjacks and whipsticks are excellent killing weapons, and in the 70s and 80s were used to kill three white Baltimoreans that I know of, used by cops. Cops are no longer supposed to use these weapons as they are exclusively used for head bashing. I cover these extensively in The Logic of Force. These cannot be legally carried in any municipality I know of. I do recommend them for home defense in tight spaces, such as hallways, bathrooms and vestibules. Hang one on the wall by your door, just don't take it outside. The nature of these weapons—unlike tools and guns—are so offensively combat specific that their possession is likely to be taken as intent.

The best hand weapon is already in your hand, and is, in my mind, the handheld mini-umbrella. Hold it by the nylon-covered wires and strike with the plastic handle. Number two would be the 14 inch 4 D-cell flashlight. You want a handy blunt weapon that is already in the hand, which means you need an excuse to have it in your hand. If you are a trained stick-fighter with contact experience then you can KO people easily with a rolled up magazine.

'The Disarming Question'

The Art of Fighting Without Fighting: Techniques of Personal Threat Evasion by Geoff Thompson

1998, Summersdale, Chichester UK, 96 pages

Geoff Thompson was a doorman in a working class English city where unarmed confrontation was a job description that sometimes produced what we in the States would call bouncers with celebrity status. To a large degree Geoff wrote about managing male-on-male ego-based confrontations in such a manner as to either diffuse them or set up the advantageous knockout of the drunken fool by the trained fighter. Geoff even wrote about boxing and scripts and expanded his original memoir style of writing into instructional videos, including an excellent book on how to kick in real situations. In essence, most of Geoff's early work focused on success in perfectly avoidable situations.

In this volume he focused more on general survival skills for the ordinary person, even women, as opposed to his original male martial artist readership. One thing that was so very telling about his work was how incredibly violent an unarmed society can be. On the other hand, this psychotic propensity for Englishmen to brawl in a near recreational capacity stilted his work toward the confrontation, where he was the practicing master. Geoff's work in this area is still relevant today, particularly in dealing with probing behavior by a person who has approached you or is barring your way, and most importantly might be using a language exchange to set you up for violence, which was the art of the English doorman, unfocusing or distracting the unruly primate with chatter precisely calibrated for the purpose of his own undoing.

The Art of Fighting Without Fighting is broken down into five chapters:

Avoidance

Escape

Verbal Dissuassion

Posturing

Restraint

A sample of his advice from the Escape chapter, that might have been titled "Latter-stage Avoidance" which included eye-contact, challenges and many other behaviors, follows:

"Often the disarming question will switch off those that are switched on. An experienced attacker will use deception to take down any defensive fences that his intended victim may have put up."

Currently, in 2016, an ocean and three decades away from where Geoff honed his skills, in a society where unarmed violence of the most brutal kind is openly permitted—even encouraged—by authorities, and the segment of the population that commits virtually all of this violence is a verbally engaged bio-mass conditioned for violence based on audio cues, his hard won advice is more applicable than ever.

'Sending their Denizens Off'

B and James on the Purposeful Destruction of White Ethnic America

Below is a Comment from the Blog posting of this Chapter, which is very well presented, followed by my impressions of two of the discussion threads, the elite war on white ethnic America and the residually related question of the plantation-era displacement of Native Americans of the Eastern Woodlands.

>Big Chev's dad was smashing skinny black restaurant staff for the crime of trying to earn a living, preserving the hierarchy of his day, promoting the reign of terror by the majority over the minority in a nation with an expanding economy.

Big Chev's dad lived in the America described in E. Michael King's Slaughter of Cities (well worth the read,) where white ethnic neighborhoods (Catholic Polish, Irish, Italian and Jewish) in cities were being destroyed by the Quaker and High Protestant elites. Why? Because these neighborhoods were a major political threat, as their populations had their own internal political institutions, disciplined vote blocks for the politicians who actually represented their communities' interests and worst of all, 3 times more kids per family than the elites. You can hear caterwauling about the Papist threat from the Eastern Protestant elites from the 1850s onwards.

The way that these neighborhoods were destroyed was through the forced importation of blacks, from the 1930s onwards (with a break from the mid-30s through the 50s.) One way was the requisitioning of private land in white neighborhoods, its clearance and the creation of projects, but this obviously required a lot of time, resources, planning and coordination. Another was to move in one black family (obviously, this would be a model family.) Then a second. Then...you know the story. Private and semi-private organizations would organize this, funded of course by the foundations. They'd try to move the first family in during the middle of the day, when the men would be at work. There was a lot of conniving from real estate brokers, who would profit massively from commissions as the whites fled.

This led to riots, so there was a hiatus for about 20 years, and then they started again in the 1950s, ultimately succeeding in breaking up these objectionable neighborhoods and sending their denizens off to assimilate in Levittowns, post-war blank cul-de-sac suburbs. Problem solved.

Big Chev's father rightly saw these blacks washing dishes as the friendly and helpful scouts and surveyors for the settling parties which would come pouring over the mountains if the former were not dealt with. They were doing the best they could to defend their families and communities.

> who literally bred the tiny indigenous population into oblivion, a population that believes in its bones and blood in quantity over quality,

Reading about the pre-1900s pioneers and settlers, I see enormous quality. For instance, Daniel Boone's family struck me as being high-quality people. The courage and gumption needed to strike westward and set up a livelihood in Indian country are certainly impressive. It's difficult for me to see the indigenous population, which apparently killed its children and old people and ate human flesh, as some sort of epigon of human quality. I mean, I can appreciate the beauty and proud bearing of a wild wolf, but I don't want to share a house or workspace with a pack of them.

Author's Response

I would like to note that the charges of planned neighborhood destruction noted by B in this comment have been overwhelmingly apparent to myself and my webmaster, Charles, as we have systematically mapped every block in Baltimore City [This project is a few weeks from publication, though the map is complete.] and rated each in terms of aggression threat and habitability. With the exception of elite enclaves in Baltimore, all upper middleclass, middleclass and working class neighborhoods, which had been built with green space intrinsic or periphery to the living space, were later targeted for subsidized housing development, with every mini-park, stand of woods, or greenway being planted with barrack-style "low rise" housing, into which criminal cadres of blacks were always moved. This was usually planned in such a way as to necessitate these introduced criminal elements traversing the middleclass area on foot to access bus lines. If the plan had really been to help the blacks, a bus line servicing employment sites would have been run to the housing site.

Satellite images of Baltimore neighborhoods appear to depict occupation and garrisoning of residential enclaves by a foreign military force.

As to the Indian versus white quantity versus quality question, the Boones and other frontiersmen essentially lives the high quality life of the Indian. Their frontier forts were modeled on palisaded Indian villages.

They dressed and hunted as Indians, not as white Europeans. They planted indigenous crops. They were the first prong of invasion. They were escaping into the wild away from the protestant elite we speak of, who then let loose the flood of low quality slave farmers to breed like rats and destroy the ecology. Boone did not stick around for this, but moved to Arkansas and hunted in the Rockies. Frontiersmen lived like Indians and hated the protestant agrarian model of life exemplified by the early Puritans like Increase Mather [Consider his first name, and the fact that—according to their own written accounts—Puritans abandoned their women and children during Indian attacks—justifying these actions with Hebrew quotes from the Old Testament—and that the Indians stayed and defended their women and young, and demonstrated the fatal weakness of loving and caring for their children!] whose book I must still review for the America in Chains project.

B, as a Hebrew scholar, you might find it of interest—and perhaps you know—that Increase Mather [the creep who founded

Harvard]and the Congregationalists of early New England, saw themselves as the real Israel, and the actual genetic Jews as traitors against God, and had every intention of building a "New Israel in the West." The Puritan brand of Christianity largely set the crux of the religion—Jesus Christ—aside, and played fanatically at being a non-Tribal counterfeit Jewish, anti-Jewish commune which I just think is disgusting—to hijack a tribal faith, appropriate the social artifices, declare your people the real tribe, and then reject every basic human notion of a tribal nature, such as respect for the warrior class.

So, to merge these two thoughts, I think in Boone and his descendents [Americans who believe in minimal government and reject social engineering], you have a westernized adaptation of the Indian way of life of the Eastern Woodlands. On the other hand, the modern, once protestant but now totally secular Anglo along with Anglo-Jewish [we can't forget those nine investment bankers that raped the nation in 2008] American elite are the real descendents of the slave masters of New England, New York, Pennsylvania and the South whose answer to disobedient white ethnic groups has been, since 1621, their replacement and displacement by imported people of other races.

I realize that I have a lot of White Nationalist readers who want to blame every problem in the world on a cradle to grave lockstep conspiracy of Jews. I however, do not believe in the Superhuman Superiority of Jews over other men as many whites do. I do not believe in a Jewish Master Race, but of a master class of manipulator, who is, by his very nature, whatever his genetic origin, a race traitor and a tribe hater. This perennial urge to lay prostrated as victim before a displaced tribe is merely feminine blame assignment rather than a masculine exercise in finding cause in order to gain an understanding.

This nation was founded by two groups of men:

To the south, nominal Catholic and Anglicans who were nothing but secular worshippers of greed...

To the North, an assortment of radical protestant cults that essentially tore the soul out of Christianity in a clearly-stated effort to recreate the idea of Israel in a heathen land by being better Jews than the actual Hebrews.

So to the argument that everything the matter with this nation can be laid at the feet of [for example] the poor Jews of Park Heights, Maryland who the rich Jew lawyers and gentile bankers threw under the black bus when I was a baby, I would remind Americans, that when your vaunted Founding Fathers had the ambition of being better Hebrews than Moses, Joshua, Samson, David and Solomon, why look for a Jew in the political woodpile when every chunk of wood in that pile aspires to being more Jewish than the real Jew?

In this writer's mind the question is essentially one of slave-masters and willing slaves conspiring to enslave that free portion of the human mind that remains to some of us on this global plantation—remembering that the English term plantation was not so-named for planting crops, but for planting people, which was the target crop all along—and how those few of us who believe in some form of transcendent aspect might at least keep the idea alive in the face of the soulless alternative, which, in the end, will erase all such tribal differences that we might get hung up on while our spiritual conquest is finalized.

Thanks, B, for your input. I promise to do an in depth review of the highly quotable and damningly honest Increase Mather book by next week. I've been swamped with writing lately and it keeps getting buried by other books in the pile.

'Just my 2 Cents'

Notes on Destroying White Ethnic Enclaves by S.S. Sam

One of our numerous bright Sams sent me this.

In your article 'Harm City East' the comment by "B" mentions a writer, E. Michael King and his book on the destruction of ethnic enclaves during the 1950's. That writer is actually E. Michael Jones, a very articulate and prolific writer with a traditional Catholic worldview. He publishes a monthly magazine, 'Culture Wars' which I've been reading for years. I recommend him highly. I'm not religious or a Catholic so am not proselytizing, but his explanations and comments on religion and culture are spot on. His work on explaining the use of blacks as the avant garde of revolution in this country is right up your alley. There are a multitude of topics he has covered that would interest you.

Just my 2 cents, Sam, the one from S...S...

Thank you, Sam.

For the readers here are the links I can find for E. Michael Jones which seem to bear on B's commentary:

http://www.culturewars.com/

http://www.bing.com/search?q=the+slaughter+of+cities+e+michael+jones&filters=ufn%3a%22the+slaughter+of+cities+e+michael+jones%22+sid%3a%22888570d0-b529-6853-3f41-b7a8b6cbb71e%22+catguid%3a%22f8f9a103-509e-90b4-1dd9-c487c3a59834_c0bcbbc4%22+segment%3a%22generic.carousel%22&FORM=SNAPST

http://www.bing.com/search?q=E+Michael+Jones+YouTube&FORM=SBRS02

https://www.darkmoon.me/2012/who-is-the-real-enemy-by-e-michael-jones/

Portrait of the Paleface Enemy

White Washington Post Reporter Laments Black Criminal Gunned Down After Burglarizing House in Liberty City

"Didn't we see this guy in the Hamilton Tavern?"

-Mescaline Franklin

Yes, he was the ski-pro from Utah with the short, snitty boyfriend.

Unfortunately, the reactionary that wrote the article below, about the liberal who wrote a Washington Proletariat article condemning some old, greedy, white bitch for unjustly shooting an innocent, unarmed black youth—who was understandably in the process of challenging the injustice of white privilege so often expressed in property rights, for the very pressing purpose of getting high—does not get it.

Paleface, the sun has set on your Race's age.

Leviathan has chosen a more compliant tool than your morally-grounded, dutiful ambition, your perverse sense of liberty and property rights upheld by a third party.

Make room!

Seriously, the reporter deserves to be staked out for the zeeks based on his hipster appearance alone. But he is simply doing his part to promote the will of the machine that owns him. He's a good slave. If you have a problem with him, your answer should not be the slave's answer of demanding that Master fix the injustice he is promoting.

It does not matter that he is of European ancestry. Race traitor-vilification is meaningless. All that matters is what race is being targeted in this cycle of Leviathan's enormous lifespan. It does not matter what ethnicity the commissar was who put you in the gulag. What matters is that you are in the gulag. Thus the value of race-traitors and other turncoat ideologues is that they serve as red herrings to direct the attention of the target group away from the machine that is gearing up to grind them to dust and encourage the doomed tribe to cast stones at one another as the gods turn their ire earthward.

It works every time.

One useful aspect of this story is that we see the purge command structure in action. When black mobs attack people of other ethnic groups, the person or persons behind the anger are always white. The enemy is untouchable. Their commands are given to the mobs by white media figures like this. If you are a paleface who wants your children to be safe in twenty years, then this media creature is the face of the enemy, promoting the will of our unseen masters to the animalistic mobs of urban—and increasingly suburban—America.

http://stuffblackpeopledontlike.blogspot.com/2016/03/white-washington-post-reporter-laments.html

'Kill Them All'

Faster with Dwayne Johnson and Billy Bob Thornton Reinforces the Social Justice Moral Hierarchy

I liked this movie, despite the subtext that I am an evil bastard for being of European descent. It did let me down in spots but was fun in a brutal, direct way.

Dwayne Johnson makes a good Arnold-Stallone upgrade and brings a lot of intensity to his part.

The movie is about a mixed-race wheel man who is released from prison and goes on a b-line rampage to avenge his brother's execution.

I like that he uses a revolver and is a direct action aggressor with no finesse.

I like that he drove a 69 Chevy Super Sport.

There was a decent knife fight in an upscale men's room.

There was an excellent emergency room execution!

The subtext delivers the following standard cultural messages which must be present in any postmodern film, and for which I forgive the filmmakers.

White kids can't play sports.

White men are evil or clueless, with any paleface not in on the scam a mere stooge on the world stage.

White men are sadistic.

White men are weaklings.

White men can't fight.

White men are cowards.

Black and mixed-race men are the models of masculinity.

White women are the smartest and most morally grounded people on the planet.

Even the most cold-blooded black criminals are honorable.

Black men care more about the impact their lifestyle choices have on their sons than do white men, who are rarely there for their sons. 'Poppa was a Rolling Stone' did not make the soundtrack cut.

Black women are the beating moral heart and strength of America.

Despite the dominance of the hip hop lifestyle in 21st century America, black life still revolves around intact nuclear families and church revivals, as it did in the 1950s.

If evil black men repent, they deserve mercy.

When evil white men repent, they deserve death.

If the mantra above disturbs you, then do not bother viewing a movie made after 2008, unless it's been banned, panned or has gone straight to video.

The Dysgenic Angels

Forget Britannia, The Statue of Liberty, Wonder Woman, Hera of the Shield, and Nike—Because Harm City Has These Whores!

Last spring, at about this time, my youngest son and I were leaving my place of employment, a supermarket, after buying steaks for breakfast. As we stepped out on the parking lot he said, "Good God, are you kidding me!"

I looked up to see three local welfare celebrities with legacy brood in tow, zooming along in a flying wing formation in three scooter chairs, the little electronic engines wound all the way out like the rotary engine Manza my best friend bought in 1978. All having the same maternal last name, their food stamps and EBT cash break on the same day, and off to market they would go.

They zoomed at 10 MPH in their Mammy State thrones, with a clutch of little albino hoodrats running along behind them, reminding one of the apobates, ancient Hellenic soldiers who held onto horse stirrups and chariot rails as they ran alongside their masters and finished off fallen foes...

These women shop regularly at that location and are rude to the staff, treating us as ill-mannered servants—and I suppose we are.

These degenerate Caucasians have a matriarch. Grandma seems to be about 60, five feet tall, with close cropped bowl cut white hair, a pot belly, and a very Down's Syndrome look to her face.

Mom #1 is in her late thirties and has some younger teens—fat girls already—scurrying behind her. She is the very spitting image of her mother, only weighing in at around 200, rather than 150, and has black hair.

Mom #2, whether she is a younger sister or a granddaughter, is unknown. She is about 21 years of age, also identical in facial appearance and equally mean to staff, but with bleached blonde hair, and weighing in at around 300 pounds, flowing over her throne, and causing her to have difficulty keeping formation, with Grandma on point. The smaller children scurry behind her, fat already at about 4 to 8 years.

Who is impregnating these hideous, retarded whores?

My point is, since the Welfare State has co-opted the Old Testament notion of being fruitful and multiplying for its own depraved purpose, the very welfare system itself seems to be geared towards producing increasingly dysgenic dependents. This is exasperated by the fact that the line of descent—being European—which has produced most scientific principals, the most conquerors, and the lunar landings of a previous age is now experiencing the lowest birthrates other than those among the most successful [in terms of innovation] Asian nation, Japan.

Is there a self-destruct mechanism in the human being that causes those populations that achieve far beyond the dreams of primal man, to dwindle, become degenerate, and even adopt anti-natal views, even as the least upward and outward looking types breed with the banal fury of rodents?

In much of his writing, Robert E. Howard conformed to the view that humanity rises from and falls back into cruder forms in cycles. My question is, could this be an inhibiter, a biological break on preventing our willful ascension from this garden of the disgraced?

'Make it Hollywood'

Notes on Our Domestication

My boss called me from a phone I would not recognize, so, when I picked up, thinking that I had won some Publishers Clearing House windfall, it was John, asking me if I'd get the dairy section ready for Good Friday, saying, "Make it Hollywood."

Well, I do not want to work an extra day and lose writing time with 74 articles on my clipboard and 4 novels in the works. But, I want John to let me have two weeks off to tramp around the Rockies in September, so I said, "Yes."

"Make it Hollywood," seems kind of hyperbolic, comparing a local grocery lineup in a working class backwater of a smallish state, to the centerpiece of global culture, to the Sacred City of the Secular World.

It does make sense. What John wanted me to do was make it look pretty, not process an order, but make something look better than it is, so that the urge to consume will take hold of the customer and increase sales.

On the surface this is to the mutual benefit of retailer and consumer. But the greatest portion of gain is had on the margin of the lie. The greater the brand loyalty of a product the less profitable to the seller and more expense to the buyer, with the manufacturer of the lie [such as Coke or Pepsi] making virtually all of the gain.

What I am merchandising is not food, not commodities, but labels, the last, least actor in a remote confidence game. Most of the dollars that flow through my hands in the form of packaged consumer goods are being spent to recover and reward advertising and labeling, to keep the consumer seduction cycle going.

For instance, the best selling yogurt is whipped with air and corn starch to affect an image of value.

The best selling cheese is not cheese, but a confection of oil, additives and dairy solids, called "cheesefood."

Of the actual cheese, yellow cheese is preferred by three out of four customers. People think that cheese is supposed to be yellow, and will argue with us all day long that it tastes different or is "bad" when white, as if cheese were made from cow's urine, not milk.

Of the cheesefoods available the national brand is priced a full dollar more and outsells the exact product [perhaps made and packed by that same company] by 4 to 1.

For every cheesefood purchase of a white cheesefood, 10 yellow purchases are made.

On the east coast only two companies pack sugar. In the mid-Atlantic market virtually all sugar is packed by the same Baltimore refinery. The store brand bricks of 4-pound sugar sometimes come mixed with the name brand as pack runs change.

Good luck convincing a customer that Domino and Richfood sugar are both packed five blocks away at the same plant.

So, I concluded by morning, as I looked at my consumable sand castle emblazoned with brand loyalty banners, if the majority of us are so easily fooled as to the substances we eat, how could we not be lead astray by these same methods, which have prepared us since childhood to act impulsively, in direct opposition to our own self-interest?

How can voting in such a consumerist matrix by anything but a sham?

A Plea for the Pallid Wee

Do WhiteTrashLivesMatter to Donorist-Capitalist-Neocon Party Bad Boy Kevin Williamson? by JOHN DERBYSHIRE

"James, a red neck old man once told me he had a special bullet for me if I ever came to see his daughter! Well Kevin Williams, I'm loading ammo for the future and we will see who goes without succor."

-Ishmael

Thanks for the head's up Ishmael.

John Derbyshire treads the ugly ground of this hidden subject quite well.

"The white underclass are the aborigines of the post-industrial age."

That quote from the article below is my favorite on the subject of American decay.

My opinion on the subject is:

Lives do not matter, only what you do with them.

If you live your own in a state of accomplishment, that matters.

If you take a life, that matters also, in its own way.

In my aboriginal post-industrial mind, taking up space does not matter, no matter what color you are.

http://www.unz.com/jderbyshire/do-whitetrashlivesmatter-to-donorist-capitalist-neocon-party-bad-boy-kevin-williamson/

'Men Who Know'

Never Trust Anyone Who Hasn't Been Punched in the Face by Scott Locklin

September 07, 2011

In this brief dose of reality, that was conveniently forgotten by most of that small portion of the world that read it, Scott Larkin exposes a truth that is so simple that it cannot possibly be true in the Land of the Lie, and that truth is simply that experience teaches.

As a writer and fight coach I have experience with false liberal delusion stemming from such beliefs born of a coddled existence as:

-There is always a rational reason for a human action.

-There is always a rational social solution to any irrational, individual, human action.

-The physical human ceiling is much lower than it is.

Scott turns some nice phrases below.

"The cause of civilizational decline is dirt-simple: lack of contact with objective reality."

"Men who have been tested physically know that inequality is a physical fact. Men who know how to deal out violence know that radical feminism's tenets—that women and men are equal—are a lie."

Consider the second quote above, in its stark, naked truth. Then consider, that the popular interpretation concerning the foundation of the United States of America essentially states the opposite.

I would like to thank Deuce for this link.

http://takimag.com/article/never_trust_any one_who_hasnt_been_punched_in_the_face/ print#axzz43wmW3iMB

'Mentally Divergent'

One of the Best Science Fiction Movies Ever Made

As a science-fiction tale 12 Monkeys is very well executed exploration of the time travel question known as the grandfather paradox.

In terms of movie making I like the Baltimore settings, loved the Philly settings, and was amazed at a film that got the best out of Willis and Pitt, whose roles I usually avoid. They both did their own brand of insane person with aplomb.

Interestingly, when people ask me—as a fight coach and violence writer—what the most realistic violence scenes in cinema are, I point to Willis' work in 12 Monkeys. From the stick up by the thugs in Philly, to the mental health restraint team, to the beating of the pimp with a phone, Bruce Willis performance as a mental case are the most realistic acts of non-military aggression I have seen in film. My favorite quotes from the film are:

"Let's go shopping, the cry of the true lunatic."

"All I see is dead people."

"Psychiatry is the latest religion."

And, yes, the cave man in me liked the leading lady, despite her lack of fleshy curves. Madeleine Stowe is my favorite skinny, cinema babe.

Most of all, 12 Monkeys is a premier dystopian view of man's lot as an occasionally striving gear in a great social machine. If you see The State as your malefactor, and you have not watched 12 Monkeys, do so.

https://www.youtube.com/watch?v=15s4Y9ffW_o

http://www.bing.com/search?q=12+monkeys+movie&form=CPDTDF&pc=CPDTDF&src=IE-SearchBox

'Two Engines of Inclusion'

The Pressure Project Podcast #223: BECOMING A BARBARIAN - JACK DONOVAN VISITS THE PRESSURE PROJECT

Master Chim and Jack dig into the rot in modern society—materialism—by discussing the fact that the all-nurturing feminine empathy ethos is in sync with corporate aggression and big money. This discussion is part of Jack's promotion of his Becoming a Barbarian.

I listened to this while writing a rape scene and listening to Mozart.

As a way of discovering how far apart your ethos is from the mainstream, listen to a five minute FM radio talk segment at 8 a.m., flip on CNN News for one segment between commercials—making sure to view the commercials—and then listen to this and see where you line up.

Jack's sense of the false emotions of the salesmen and the disgusting customer service retail matrix so many of us exist in is on point.

Master Chim seems to have an excellent mindset for a martial arts school leader and finding out he is New York-based, I hope to line up some cross-training or competition with our Maryland and PA fighters.

https://www.youtube.com/watch?v=mFs-hcWOvps

'A Punk Overmatched'

Two Black on White Mob Attacks That Failed

"This is a both a good realistic visualization exercise scenario and a bit of entertainment seeing a punk overmatched."

-Mescaline Franklin

Black People Pick on Wrong Homeless Guy—Former NFL Player Chris Brymer

In this video we see one of the methods of black on white violence, which is to support and bitch-cheer on the biggest, toughest guy in your group, a guy who can fight and may even come wearing driving, MMA or boxing gloves. The man behind the video phone should be credited with a modicum of decency for pointing out that this was a

Knockout Game production and not the more serious type of black on white mob attack, which is more cohesive, discouraging an escalation.

The more cohesive type of attack may or may not be more injurious. It really comes down to whether or not the defender fights back and then if he can take out the attackers. In this case, if the target of the attack had been smaller, older, less athletic, he may have been seriously hurt. The point behind this type of attack is legalistic. These are people who come from a population that has been targeted by the law enforcement apparatus for 40 years, and have learned how to game it. They know that the most important ingredient in an act of violence is to have a witness sympathetic to your cause to make sure you don't do any time with 'real niggas' for your primate proclivities on the streets.

In terms of my violence survey, this is an indecisive resolution as neither side imposed their will.

https://www.youtube.com/watch?v=j2lKdoc2PT4

Black mob in Houston chooses wrong white guy. Sorry.

Below is an example of poor prey selection exposing a common pack hunting tactic. Like all advanced predators, American hoodrats work in teams, with support and contact elements.

https://www.youtube.com/watch?v=wsJer3KY-wA

'Apothegm'

West of Eden by Harry Harrison

The first in a trilogy continued by Winter in Eden and Return to Eden, this brilliant book supposes that the dinosaurs were never wiped out and that when primates evolved into humans they did so based on New World primates. Intelligent saurian scientists come to the Western hemisphere and discover that intelligent mammals bar their way. The Eden series is perhaps my favorite science-fiction trilogy. The best aspect of the alternate universe was that Harrison supposed that instead of embracing technology, the saurian scientists become biologists, breeding plants and animal to fulfill functions that humans would construct tools for. Their vessels are modified leviathans, their weapons are mutated lizards that spit poison darts, mutated frogs have been bred to the point that they serve as optical devices...

Harry Harrison crafted a masterful alternative reality in only three books and I found it endlessly fascinating. The narrative embraces an alien view of humanity, as well as the human view of an awful invader. The Eden trilogy is, above all, the struggle of native people resisting an alien invader, and makes light—and politically veiled—for any primate concerned with maintaining his viability in his native land.

http://www.audible.com/pd/Sci-Fi-Fantasy/West-of-Eden-Audiobook/B00TRPZI2Y

https://en.wikipedia.org/wiki/West_of_Eden

'With Our Mother's Milk'

Joe Rogan Experience #725 - Graham Hancock & Randall Carlson

Thanks to Sam J. and others for convincing me to view this. Three hours is a lot of time for me to part with, but I did, with a little help from my friend Mister Molson. I know he's Canadian, but my grandmother Alberta Roy was too, and that is where the comet hit, right?

"Thank you, Jupiter."

It is interesting that Jupiter [Zeus] was the god of lightning and thunder that threw death and disaster down into the mortal world, and was pretty free with his semen, and that the planet Jupiter has taken more comets for the solar team than we would care to dream of.

The excellent aspect of this podcast is the fact that our current culture's obsession with the earth, which Graham calls "earth-centric" is essentially emasculating. Astronomy was once the province of men, the fields of the women. We are now emasculated on a cosmic level. Imagine sitting on a floating island and being unconcerned with the other floating islands? That is how inward-looking and masturbatory our current human viewpoint is.

The dogma of archaeology discussed by Graham Hancock is very familiar to a reader of War before Civilization *'The Pain Of Being Human'*. Graham's appreciation of the Iliad, and the Gate of Horn in his discussion of dreams with dope-head Rogan, does get us closer to the ancient mindset—which was so stoner friendly it makes puritans—and even catholic-spawned drunks like me—shiver in dread, as I down another brew, thank you. All puns aside dreams—and the illness of epilepsy—was very important to the ancients, who were generalists, which makes appreciation of their view difficult for us, who hold so much fragmentary evidence that we have difficulty synthesizing it.

https://www.youtube.com/watch?v=1cbnCr HwVSg

Yomageddon

A Half Million Entitled Social Justice Heroes to be Martyred Today!

"No joke: 500k food stamp recipients to lose benefits on April 1.

Just thought you should know. Batten down the hatches."

-Travolta

https://www.rt.com/usa/337926-americans-food-stamps-benefits/

Thanks, Bro. I know you are glad to be out of retail food for good.

From my reading of this the effect is going to be primarily on junkies and other lowlife forms, who will amp up shoplifting and panhandling and burglary. The welfare mammas and their vast broods will not be touched. The two populations of adults hit with this are going to be 20-something slackers and 50-something losers—mostly palefaces—the first group mostly addicts, the second group mostly being pushed out of the workplace by younger competition. The second group is mostly going to roll over and die and the first group is already causing trouble, so I think the result in supermarkets is going to be felt mostly by loss prevention operatives as an escalation of existing theft patterns and by the rest of us as more aggressive panhandling.

This will not be Yomaggedon, but a baby step toward eventual welfare-cutting measures that must eventually happen as the economy continues along its course, and will, in the end, spark more aggressive looting behavior. Do note that once looting occurs across a community, the looters discover how powerless the police are, and will continue looting activity at lower intensity indefinitely, which has happened in Baltimore, where much shoplifting is now indistinguishable from small scale looting.

'Raped by Burning Fire Sticks'

Zombie Apocalypse Mutant Biker Fighters by Eirik Bloodaxe

© 2016 James LaFond

I have promised Eirik to revisit his vast book on neo-barbarism monthly. So here it is, another reason why Eirik—who cannot write under his real name for fear of persecution—will hopefully get this book in print. 36 pages in we are still in the introduction discussing the metaphysics and physics of cultural collapse. Unfortunately Eirik points out proof that aboriginal men are vicious to their women, which is puzzling, since we in the West understand that spousal abuse is the exclusive province of white men.

Below is a quote from page 36 of this amazingly detailed, dark document on the failing state of the human condition in the Western World, with associated footnotes.

"In Australia, Aboriginal women are 80 times more likely to be hospitalized for assault and injury than women in the rest of the population. According to one mainstream article: "[m]any of the assaults are perpetrated by the women's husbands or partners and include being raped with wooden or metal objects, or being murdered by being repeatedly punched and struck with a saucepan, stones, a wheel rim and a wheel brace." Aboriginal women have also been raped by burning fire sticks. The issue of violence against Aboriginal women and children was raised by Aboriginal Northern Territory MP Bess Price, who has said that she has been "routinely attacked" and "obscenely insulted" by the "progressive left and its comfortably middle class urban Indigenous supporters." This is all part of an enormously complex social problem, with no easy solution, arising from a fundamental clash of cultures."

The footnote citations are at the end of this review.

I highly recommend Eirik's work and am hoping he will write something for this site about his experiences in a western nation that we in the U.S. don't hear a lot from in terms of cultural collapse.

Footnotes

"Violence against Aboriginal Women 80 Times Worse," June 10, 2013, at http://www.news.com.au/national/violence-against-aboriginal-women-80-times-worse/story-e6frfkp9-1226661209335.

As above. See further: T. Thomas, " 'Yabbered' to Death – Part I," Quadrant, May 6, 2013, at http://quadrant.org.au/opinion/bennelong-papers/2013/05/yabbered-to-death-part-i/; Stephanie Jarrett, Liberating Aboriginal People from Violence, (Connor Court, Ballan, 2013); P. Sutton, The Politics of Suffering, (Melbourne University Publishing, Carlton, 2011).

'The Unmindful'

The Ultimate Dystopian Fact Book by Eirik Bloodaxe

Chapter 1 of Eirik Bloodaxe's book on neo-barbarism, Zombie Apocalypse Mutant Biker Fighters, constitutes the most comprehensive discussion of the zombie mythos of various human cultures I have been exposed to. His level of research is invigorating, and I found myself reading his work instead of doing mine, and have thus popped out what should have been May's review of his work today—this is just great stuff. Eirik includes an extensive look at zombies in film for you video nerds out there, but keeps coming back to the fact that the "unmindful" human masses that the ancient Greek Heraclitus warned us of are all around us.

He even examines the hours-long, hundred-man rape of CBS news liberal babe Lara Logan by Egyptian men, which begs the question who is the zombie, this stupid broad or the men? She is, after all, behaving as a news correspondent precisely in the character of the female victims in slasher flicks, who walk rabbit like into the jaws of predators, psychologically enabled in this by their belief in the most toxic liberal version of the lie that is civilization. A truthful look at the Katrina disaster, as examined by Eirik, that was lied about and mythologized in opposite ways by the Right and the Left, makes a good case for predicting future disaster aftermaths and compensating mythology.

I can tell you this, no horror movie depicting black men raping white women as it did occur after Katrina will ever be made while our current social structure continues as it is, which, is in itself evidence of the "unmindful" state of civilization.

Thanks for the review copy, Eirik, I'm enjoying it quite a lot.

'Once You Get on the Bus'

Old White Dude Attacked by black people on bus. No big deal.

"Even more chilling is the video in the elevator Colin adds at the end. The woman had to deal with a far more dangerous attacker then the white man/punching bag. Even Colin does not feel too sorry for him."

-Mescaline Franklin

A fair number of white men who use mass transit have health and neurological conditions that prevent them from either earning enough money to buy a car or defend themselves. The way he is standing, letting someone under his chin, was a flag that he could be taken down with no risk.

Briefly, if I get threatened like this on the bus, I will stab every human being on that bus at least once, and they will be rip cut stabs, difficult to stitch. I've run it through my head hundreds of times on the bus. I can stick thirty people in 25 seconds, not a problem.

Look at the second video in the last 25 seconds and you will see the body language that denotes a setup attack. No white woman should be alone in urban America. Beyond that, this happens to men too. Study this film and visualize punching his ear in and then smashing him into the wall, pinning his right hand. It will always be the right hand. Keep it from coming out of the pocket, because there may be something in it. Once he is immobilized keep wrestling for that knife. Don't use the knife on him, but continue to attack his hand, snapping off his fingers between your hands and if you begin losing control of his hand poking and gouging his eyes. Note that this is a racist attack, with no robbery motive, simply an attempt to gut a white person.

https://www.youtube.com/watch?v=3H_DX-MiX5Q

'Break out the Natty Boh'

A Missive from Mescaline Franklin

"I remember the story with the little girl from a few years ago, so now the guy who tried to abduct her gets dealt with. Break out the Natty Boh! Thank goodness for the police. That Korean woman has more guts than over half of Murican men."

-Mescaline

Thanks, Mescaline.

This is not just a video, but a news story spliced from various videos.

I remember how disgusted I was to find out my Vietnamese lady friend Miss Lilly had been tortured and robbed in her father's Belair-Edison store by a black cop while a black hoodlum looted snack food and sodas.

I love how the pigs side with the violent black criminals against the Asian shopkeepers. The cops leave these two peaceful Asians under siege and then come down on the criminal's side.

Do I have to say it?

Do you really want me to quote Ice Cube?

Be prepared, one day the police and black thugs will be shoulder to shoulder wiping out Asians and whites.

It's coming.

The first shots were fired in Baltimore last year, cops looking the other way while we were hunted.

It is only a matter of time before the pigs join the hunt.

Okay—Fuck the Police.

https://www.youtube.com/watch?v=wefUbN zzonE

Chore Boy

The Moral Complicity of Conservative America

I have written much of how the American Left, the liberals, have undermined society—particularly the masculine virtues of Western society—in the name of a greater good that they claim is moral rather than material, yet is utterly an expression of decadent materialism. Libertarians might call such bad results "the soul-tax due to the God of Unintended Consequences." But to look at the liberal Left I see intent, intent to destroy manhood and free will and see nothing unintended about it. A few weeks ago, discussing politics past with an older man, I had to restrain myself when he referred to William F. Buckley as "representing the American Right."

Ever since then I've been wondering if what reamins of moral America would give me a clue as to the method of indicting what passes for the Right in America. Yes, the liberals, the Left, the Democrats have intentionally destroyed the residual ethos of an older society which was based on building and have replaced it with a society based on destruction at every level, with the targeted destruction of the nuclear family ushering in an age of fatherless brutality.

The night before last I walked into work to clock in and saw the annual sorrow story that is the countertop quarter donation board for Saint Jude's Children's Hospital, featuring Baby Joshua recovering from blood cancer. The board has been pillaged by local dope fiends and the taped-in quarters have been ripped out, every minor theft caught on security video. Then, when I enter the dock to unplug the tow-motor, I see what every grocer who enters a receiving area sees when his eyes falls on the outgoing boxes of damaged merchandise: boxes of Chore Boy brass scrubbing pads, which are ripped into by the fiendish claws of the inhuman creatures known as crack-heads for the buffering of their make-shift pipes. 20% of this product, designed for cleaning kitchenware, will be destroyed on the shelf by crack-heads, a toxic parasite directly engineered by the American Right, in its wrong-headed drug war.

As drug addiction proliferates among the lower class of the majority ethnic group as the young of a politically correct nation whose hopes have been outsourced attempt to numb themselves with drugs designed to survive the Drug War, their very existence serves as a crutch for the Left. From the point of view of someone who hates civilization the fact that the dispossessed must seek designer intoxicants rather than natural compounds in their bid to escape the insanity of the Mother State is confirmation that the Right and the Left are simply two arms of the same obscene, mind-screwing organism.

Felling Faggot Foes

A Boxer's Mob Attack Answer

The type of emasculated, girly-yos that form most modern mobs, when they attack a hard case, are primarily a legal threat.

If you pull a knife they scatter and call the pigs.

If you drop one the rest call the cops and witness against you concerning your unsolicited attack.

If you start lunging for them they will bounce and dart like the sissies they are, go get reinforcements and break out their smartphones to video your aggression.

Let them hit you. If one hits you another may try, which brings multiple targets into your wheelhouse. Practice the following combination while standing, just to ingrain this body mechanic into your survival arsenal. This is something that you would rarely do in the ring and never in the cage, but against feather-fisted fag-foes on the sidewalks of Unmanly America it is a good unarmed option. Train this five punch combo in the mirror, in the closet, in the shower and on the bag.

One: A power pivot jab landing high with a three quarter fist.

Two: A straight right to the body, fully pronated, with a sinking knee drop that will shift weight to the left leg, the knee of which should bend.

One: An up-jab, powered by a pivot as the knee straightens out, driving with your thing up into the chin, landing with a palm-up supinated fist

Two: A classic straight right with three-quarter fist driving off the rear foot with that meaty Caucasian calf!

One: A spear-hand jab, driving your coned fingers—with the thumb and pinkie acting as under-braces—into that oppressed eye-socket!

Repeat as necessary.

Any high line shots that are uncertain might be thrown as controlling slaps to fix the target and crack it with the next punch, as all of these are power shots.

Reaping Urban Wheat

The Knife Stroke That Will Stop the Serious Attacker

© 2016 James LaFond

There are various levels of attacks launched at us palefaces and Neanderthals by the minions of the State. The worst are currently attacks by 3-5 innocent, unarmed, adult black males using a car for mobility. One of these Yos will have a pocket knife and bottles and curb chunks will become part of any escalation of force used by these martyrs of American Liberalism against a determined defender.

This is why I carry a knife, to deal with such a threat as this.

To avoid felony conviction for the crime of defending yourself against these victims of your oppression, do not:

-Stab repeatedly as this is a prison assassination method

-Do not slash their wrists or hands. Although this is FMA doctrine, it can be claimed by your attacker as evidence that he was just defending himself.

-Do not strike the face with the blade as some states have additional charges for maiming and disfiguring.

-Do not slash or stab the neck area.

If you are attacked by a mob of adult men, or if you are a woman being attacked by an adult male, do:

-Grab the attacker in front of you with your left hand. A handful of hoody will do.

-Use a hammer grip, not a saber or rapier or reverse grip. Hold onto this sucker.

-Stab into his guts, just below the ribs, with a pronated thrust, with your palm facing down, the thumb and index finger of your knife hand punching into his belly.

-Twist the blade into a thumb-up hammer-grip position and rip-cut down until you hit bone, holding tightly to him

-Having run your blade into his hip bone or pelvis, turn your blade palm up, and in supination rip-cut across his lower abdomen as you continue to hold him—shelling up your shoulders and tucking your chin to keep the strikes of his friends from hitting your chin.

-As you execute this exit rip-cut, which will disable but not kill him, keep travelling to your left and lurch into the next attacker, grabbing him as you slam your blade in pronation, into his guts, just below the ribs...

Make sure not to stab higher than the bottom rib as this could strike the heart and kill him.

Do not stab him in the outside of the leg as you are likely to lose the knife when he starts jumping around.

Do not stab him on the inside of the leg as this could cause him to bleed out and die.

If the angle is wrong for you to stroke higher than the waist—for instance you have been knocked to one knee—then slam that knife into his groin and do a vertical downward rip-cut, getting your knife hand out from between his soon to be clinching legs immediately.

Don't finish anyone with the blade.

If a dude is trying to get off the floor even after getting rip-cut, he is probably armed, so jump high in the air and land with both boot heels on his head. Note that this will not be legally defensible unless you have already shanked one or more yos and you have been hit. It is offered here as a desperate alternative to finishing a foe with the knife when you have been injured and other foes are still actively seeking your demise and this guy is potentially introducing a weapon.

Notice the unseen enemy, the prejudicial, criminal-loving referee from Hell who will be judging you in hindsight from the comfort of her bench. Remember, in your preparations for defense, that she is your ultimate enemy, an all-powerful enemy who must be outwitted.

The Price of Leviathan Oil

Nero the Pict Gives Us a Pre-Apocalyptic Heads Up

"You might wanna give this podcast a listen. Don't know if you are familiar with Peak Oil theorist James Howard Kunstler. This is a conversation with a 21st century world traveling Booker T by the name of Christopher Cornelius that you might enjoy listening to. It rambles but bear it out. His rah rah USA trip is a little painful but also true in spots:"

KunstlerCast 276 - That Conversation About Race We Were Supposed to Have - ...

"Christopher Cornelius" is the nom de guerre of a black American international humanitarian aid worker who has...

http://kunstler.com/podcast/kunstlercast-276-conversation-race-supposed/

Take care, brother man,

Nero the Pict

'The Restructuring of Society'

The Biggest Scam In United States History | G. Edward Griffin and Stefan Molyneux

If you have not heard of the fractionary reserve system this video is a low-friction entry. If you are a Peak Prosperity reader or Zeitgeist viewer the scope of this subject is known to you. If not you should view this. If so, pay attention to the pop-up menu at the top of the screen which gives links to more specific videos and enjoy all of the nerdish details about how the executioner's hood was pulled over our great grandparent's head as we were sold into slavery generations before our birth.

One early crusader against central banking was Andrew Jackson, who will one day pay for this sin by having his face removed from the $20 bill issued by the monster he hoped would never rise again—or was that the punishment and will his ultimate post-mortem vilification equal the freeing of his shackled shade?

A book that explains how this fraud is committed is Confessions of an Economic Hitman, reviewed here: *Our Pound Of Flesh*

https://www.youtube.com/watch?v=dsqGR3 1zoVA&nohtml5=False

'Reverting to Type'

Guest Author Lynn D. and James Discuss African Descent

One of your recent posts has a list of policy suggestions that I have forwarded to my congressional representatives (haha). One of the items is that at least part of the benefits need to go to the father. This suggestion has been made by another crackpot I read here:

https://westhunt.wordpress.com/2015/05/26/when-public-policy-meets-elementary-biology/

Unfortunately, that crackpot died a few days ago. He was a college professor and seemed like a nice guy, Henry Harpending. His writing partner, Greg Cochran, yet lives and is a big Robert E. Howard fan. These two predicted that modern humans carry Neanderthal genes long before the discovery was made, among many other interesting and accurate predictions and observations. Cochran seems to think the African Bushmen may not be technically human.

Harpending spent a lot of time in Africa and wrote a little of his experience, for example here:

https://westhunt.wordpress.com/2012/06/02/ethnographic-surprises-i-the-child-bride/

He gives an example of a fairly matriarchal sub-Saharan African group. His writing and other sources lead me to believe that our own beloved Africans are reverting to type, with welfare benefits standing in for the ease of food cultivation in Africa, contrary to northern latitudes, where hunting is required for survival and farming requires heavier labor, making men the main bread- (and meat-) winners. I think the period between slavery and the civil rights movement represents a time when European lifestyles were impressed upon Africans, contrasted with the post civil rights era, when the African lifestyle is praised and encouraged through public policy.

This is a good story about his experience hunting a cape buffalo, perhaps relevant to your upcoming western adventure:

http://the10000yearexplosion.com/henry-and-the-cape-buffalo/

Congratulations on your Baltimore mapping project, I hope never to need it!

I am interested to see your comments as well.

Thanks,

Lynn D.

The Cracked Pottery of an Opinion

Thanks for this, Lynn.

I will respond before reading the links and read them afterward as I'm interested in the divergence of opinion between myself and the authors linked above. I'm hoping to find something in these pieces to expand my understanding and may review them separately in the future.

One place that we really cannot generalize about ethnographically is Africa, as there is a wider genetic range among Africans than the rest of the world combined, which has something to do with the Bottleneck Event caused by the Toba Super Eruption 74,000 years ago. We also have to be careful about considering our African Americans, who came from West Africa from Angola to Nigeria, but mostly along the Gold Coast. If we look at this portion of West Africa we find one nation, Dahomey, that had a form of Matriarchy, similar to what my black friends call "the White Daddy government" in which black women have the upper hand in the black sub culture because they have been granted a monopoly on raising young men, are the conduit for government subsidies to their community, and enjoy preferential treatment for criminal activity compared to their men. A co-worker of mine recently went to a wedding in Jersey, where her cousin, a woman who was recently released after doing five years for murdering her husband, was getting married to her next victim.

In Dahomey the king had a lousy army of poorly trained, fed and motivated men, who melted before the French Foreign Legion. His body gaurds—5,000 amazons—fought well, for they were not only the king's elite bodyguard, but his harem as well. In addition to the privilege of pleasuring the king, these women could take wives and head households.

If there is more of a propensity to accepting this false matriarchy—which is really a centralized patriarchy—among people of direct, recent African descent, perhaps it has to do with the fact that men have always led explorations. Women may sometimes lead nations to war, but men are ever the explorers. Therefore, populations who managed to escape Africa—no small feat as it involved transiting the Sahara—would be more patriarchal at their root. However, the majority of African cultures are intensely patriarchal, especially in East Africa.

As for the bushmen or !Kung, previously known as "Cappoid" for their unique hair, and whose women have additional labial flesh and increased fat storage capacity in their rear end, they dominated Africa for most of the last 20,000 years, and were only gradually displaced by the black tribes after Malaysian seafarers introduced the yam and iron working [which was also introduced from Egypt, earlier but to less widespread effect] around A.D. 500. Eventually these people were driven into the southwestern portion of Africa where they were caught in a vice between the Bantus, the Dutch, and later the Germans in Namibia, who all hunted them like animals. These people had managed to adapt to desert conditions without camels and other livestock and suffered much from the introduction of the horse and camel into the Sahara. I have only read three books on the Cappoid race and wonder about much more than I can recall. They seem to be the real life counterpart of Robert E. Howard's fantastical Picts, a race apart who saw civilizations rise and fall and still managed to hang on—though their days appear to be close to an end. If a comet hit the planet, though, next week, for instance, I'd put them in the front running for being around when the next ice age waxed wroth.

As for the astonishing level of violence among modern African Americans compared to others, the fact that the white elite deny it, and the underlying reality that most of the black violence targets peaceful blacks, all I can determine is that the people heading our ship of state want black violence—including black-on-black violence—to continue. So, although blacks seem to act more violently under the same circumstances as other types of people, we can't take the European influence off the table yet, as African Americans yet live under the thumb of, study at the knee of and rage at the command of, upper class Americans of European descent.

'Within Heathenry'

Forging the Hero by John Mosby: A Start The World Podcast with Jack Donovan

John Mosby carries the name of the greatest partisan of the Confederate States of America who was a blood enemy of George Armstrong Custer during the Civil War. John is an authentic rural rifleman, a type of man who I rate as the lineal cultural descendents of the Native American warriors that their kind fought for hundreds of years. It is fascinating that the real gritty expression of pre-Christian European tribalism is being carried by Americans of recent Christian lineage, with the secular humanist seemingly continuing the separation of the early European ideals from its bloodline. In my view, the primal ideal of life is most lively in America among men of European descent who are simultaneously keeping alive native warrior traditions [deer hunting was not a European tradition] and ancient European values.

I really like the way in which John makes certain to get beyond the rudimentary "in-group" "out-group" idea of tribalism that is the crude construct of post-moderns clutching for a misunderstood past, and speaks on inter-tribal tribalism and gradual decline. John is not some meathead military guy, but an educated historian.

Checkout this interesting podcast at the link below.

http://www.jack-donovan.com/axis/2016/04/stw-episode-13-john-mosby-forging-the-hero/

'Pampered Toy Dogs of Victimland'

An Echo in the Man Cave from Adam

"The pampered toy dogs of Victimland are turning on themselves, and the whole affair makes me sick to my stomach."

-Adam

Micro-aggressions?

Is that when the guy can't hit hard or when he is a rapist with micro-penis?

I really like this victimhood stuff. To be surrounded by grievance whores is empowering.

The demise of honor culture is the demise of Man. So, hopefully this blooming victim culture will do away with our third-party proxy-aggressor dignity culture.

The "good us" and "evil them" tribal instincts of ours has ever been the collective neck about which the leash of State is clasped.

https://youtu.be/10B9Fc8BmR0

Run Whitey, Run

Outtakes from the Invasion of White Marsh

© 2016 James LaFond

When I moved to Baltimore in the early 1980s White Marsh was the hub of white flight. The people that originally fled Baltimore in the early 1980s have paid off their houses in the past five years, and have hosted a large influx of hipster types moving into the McMansions and upscale townhomes erected around the White Marsh Mall and The Avenue at White Marsh commercial centers right off of Interstate-95 over the past 10 years.

Over the past five years there has been another influx: subsidized housing in White Marsh has brought hundreds of welfare families from Baltimore City ghettos into this middleclass Baltimore County area. During the Race Purge of April 2015 there was no activity of note in White Marsh, with Rosedale, to the south and technically part of the White Marsh police precinct, bearing the brunt of black-on-white mob violence. However, this spring, and this past winter, White Marsh has been the stick-up capital of Baltimore County, with home invasions— never reported as such by the Baltimore County Pig Department—recently joining the operational template of Baltimore County black-on-white crime.

Below are examples from this past week of surging violent crime in an area that was free of it up until a few years ago:

4/5/16, 9:37 a.m., Roseland Avenue two black youths invaded a house, attacked the occupant, looted the electronics and fled. This was a home invasion, but is not being reported as such.

4/8/16, 9:45 p.m. St. Regis Road, a pizza delivery man was stuck-up by an innocent, unarmed, black youth, who never-the-less had a handgun. The driver had no money and was not harmed

4/10/16, 2:30 a.m. Ebenezer and Fieldchat [a rural area], two blacks dismounted from a car and robbed a white man at gunpoint, and then remounted and drove off, apparently resuming their patrol

During this same week there was an armed home invasion a mile south in Rosedale and numerous burglaries in White Marsh. The burglaries cannot be racially assigned. However they were rare when it was an all white neighborhood.

If you live in such a suburban area, where government mandated subsidized housing is ongoing, the incidence of handgun robberies and burglaries reported by police will increase. However, mob beatings will not be reported, except by citizens on social media, and all home invasions will be reclassified as burglaries and assaults.

The Three Little People

When the Hoodrat Wolf-Pack Huffs and Puffs and Threatens to Blow Your Door In

Yesterday, at 5:30 p.m., I was headed up to the gym, cutting through the Ridgely Oak neighborhood, when, walking up White Oak to Oak, I saw a group of 20-30 older teen and adult blacks, evenly mixed between male and female. I noticed the males as I was behind and they were the support element. The victims and neighbors noticed the females.

I had a friend check on social media with the neighborhood association and have a rough understanding of what transpired before and after I made a right up Oak and passed a county pig cruising toward the scene. Currently this neighborhood is only 15% black, yet they own the streets as the sissy whites wonder what is happening. The social media posts indicate a total incomprehension of black urban culture. The media has prepped these victims well.

I do not know if the specific victims were white, and based on media posts, am guessing that they are not, because they seemed to know what was what, unlike the neighbors who were shocked. If they were white or black does not matter. If decent blacks move into your neighborhood and you do not have men to defend them from the gangs that will root them out so that they can be your residential predators, then you are next.

The daughter has been subject to attacks at school and has been pulled from Loch Raven Senior High.

The predators Googled her house address and showed up in masse to stage a home invasion, led by an adult woman. These teen males were on average six feet and 180 pounds.

The parents were at work.

The rest of the information is hazy.

The two grandfathers showed up to defend the house, apparently unarmed. One was stricken down and four mob members breached the front door and were able to lay hands on the girl.

Police arrived, with one cop falling on the sidewalk as the mob fled.

Police and neighbors are suggesting assault charges, where this was clearly a blatant home invasion.

I have, in the past, been in this situation.

If you are in this situation do not open your door to communicate with the besiegers. Moral authority does not apply to mob attacks.

If you must open the door to retrieve a family member do not do so unarmed and do not rely on a blunt weapon, which is of limited value against a mob. Appear with an edged weapon or firearm, making sure to advance only enough to bring in your kin. Do not attempt to drive off the besiegers. Such sorties are frowned on by the Police State, which is first and foremost concerned with the rights of your attackers and the prospect of you using a weapon.

Get back inside as soon as possible. If the cops see you on the lawn with a weapon, you may be one of the roughly 500 whites killed by cops this year as opposed to the approximately 200 blacks killed by cops in the same period of occupation.

If you have two men, the strong one should hold the door and push back, while the other uses a weapon—such as a butcher knife or fireplace poker—on whatever attacker manages to breach the open portion of the door.

This is why sensible city dwellers, when hunkering down, always install barred security storm doors that open outward and have heavy inside doors that open toward a wall that your back can be braced against while your partner butchers those hoodrats who squeeze through to get their huminary cheese.

Note that this is a suburb that working and middle class city folks resettled to when they were driven from Baltimore decades ago. The State is now sending their moral chattel across the DeYoified Zone to root at the children of those who escaped.

Below is the link to a house listed for sale within two blocks of the attack. There are multiple sale signs on every block. The tide has risen and the inner dykes are breached. The fight will now be house to house.

This was a Black Spring Tactical Strike in one of the Baltimore County neighborhoods I am studying as the hunt for palefaces and colored sympathizers intensifies. Do note that the neighborhood association was told by the police that they do not always have "the resources" to send out an officer on such calls. The cops seem to be using a counter-surge strategy.

https://www.coldwellbankerhomes.com/md/baltimore/8529-oak-road/pid_11508646/

Afterward

The felons have announced that they will be back and know well that the police cannot provide protection. The commentary by the local whites about how the adult female was setting a bad example show astounding ignorance. That bitch was setting a good example, training up a click on behalf of some other, more influential, woman operating behind the scenes. She is probably the aunt of one of the attackers.

'Don't Let Me Beat You Down'

A Letter to Hard Times Readers

Yesterday I was forwarded a discussion concerning my "blog" as a self-help resource from a site called redit. I often forget that I am primarily used as a self-help writer, probably because I have no such ambition, but have often fallen into the trap of writing for others.

Both of these readers were positive about the style and content of my writing. However, the more expressive reader has felt—in various posts—that I had been beating him down. He had apparently fallen on hard times and was seeing himself in a negative light to begin with and some of my irony was too depressing for him to get past. He still recommended my writing for readers looking to improve themselves with the caveat that they should wait sometime and get over their own negative feelings about themselves before delving into my well of irony.

Let me be clear here, I write self-help for those areas I coach in: boxing, stick-fighting, knife-fighting and machete dueling and also in response to various questions concerning writing and dating for those masochists with the poor judgment to ask.

I'm not a cheerleader.

I'm not writing to help anyone, but express my odd view of the world which is utterly unwelcome amongst those I am in day-to-day contact with.

Please, if you are kind enough with your time to spend some of it reading my doomed opinion, don't let me get you down. Just laugh and say, "Only seventy-one out of eight-billion people agree with him—and he's an asshole! Crowds of black men used to part and make way as he prowled through their hood. Now the local hoodrats think he's Santa Claus. I might have it bad, but at least I'm not James LaFond!"

Coming to Harm City on Business?

An Action Plan for Paleface Prey

Lynn, a reader who has contributed to the site and had previously reveled in the fact that she would never need the Baltimore Travel Guide, just discovered that her husband is coming to Baltimore for business next week and although he is staying in a hotel just inside the blue zone, he is working firmly in the red zone! She sent off an e-mail to me yesterday wanting some advice for her patriarch.

The Hotel

1. Arrange for a private cab or sedan at the cab stand out front—usually the oldest African man is the guy you want or a Sikh— or through the hotel manager or desk clerk.

2. The only after-work socializing should be done at the hotel, or close by with a group of coworkers who are also returning to the hotel, not going elsewhere.

3. Do not get cozy with any Eastern Europeans that might frequent the hotel lounge. There are Russian prostitutes working out of the hotel he is staying in, Lynn. They seem like nice girls, but the guys that handle them give me the creeps.

4. Do not use public transportation unless it is the circulator [which runs in four colored lines on 15-minute cycles around the Hotel Zone] busses, which are much safer and free than the MTA buses, which should be avoided.

5. Be inside the hotel before night. Basically pretend you are in a vampire flick directed by a bloodthirsty 16-year old.

The Red Zone Work Site

1. Residential: it will be mildly dangerous during the day, with muggings and stickups

likely, and a death trap at night. If he is doing social work he should really call it a day at 1:30 so that he is not spotted by the mobs of violent felons being released from schools, who make the afternoon from 2-6 more dangerous than the summer hours of dusk.

2. Commercial: a pain in the ass during the day due to panhandlers and a prime hunting ground for packs of hoodrats at night. If he is doing a supermarket set tell him to leave with the manager, but not to hit the bar with the manager.

3. Industrial/medical: perfectly safe on site at all times with some security outside during the day. This could be walked to—so long as it does not take you through residential—during the day. But, at night will feature less frequent but more dangerous predation than commercial zones. Johns Hopkins hospital will provide armed security escorts to the parking garage!

4. Government: during the day the interior and exterior is as safe as any place in suburban America. However, if you get

caught outside at dusk, lookout. People get attacked right outside the police precinct parking garage all the time and the City Courthouse is a full blown human imitation of a Wild Kingdom episode at night. At night, unoccupied government building exteriors are extremely dangerous. If he is working at one of these places make like it's a vampire movie and boogie before dusk.

5. Do not ever walk or bus home from the job, but have an arrangement with a driver.

6. If, somehow, he is caught on foot in the red zone at night, wave frantically for a cab. I have numerous accounts in my notes of cabbies saving palefaces from danger, with some of them reading like military rescue missions.

If Unrest Erupts?

Lynn, I do not mean to be hyperbolic, but we are 12 days from the Harm City Race Purge anniversary, and the hoodrat brain is already geared toward remembering annual dates, as exemplified by the fact that more food stamp dollars go to decorative birthday cakes than any other food item.

Stay inside the hotel for as long as the unrest is ongoing.

If he gets caught in an outlying area, have him give me a call at 443-686-0598. The voice mail is broken. So if I don't answer, text me. I'm not Cull of the Nords, but I'll see what I can do.

Cecil

Coming Clean in Harm City

Cecil is 26, medium height, athletic build, with sandy blonde hair and a handsome face. He wears jeans, a polo shirt, lives in a halfway house on White Avenue and attends the rehab clinics and Narcotics Anonymous meetings at the various churches on Harford Road.

I'm up from Florida, still have the Florida I.D. My dad kicked me out—got tired of me stealing all of his stuff for drug money. I'm from Baltimore County. My mom kicked me out last year for steeling all of her stuff and pawning it.

Now, Florida is a great place to get high, plenty of heroin and other drugs in Florida. But they don't have any rehab down there. People ask me why I would come back to the

East Coast—to Baltimore to get clean—and I tell them it's because Baltimore has the heroin and the rehab, whatever you need, where Florida just has the heroin.

I need to get clean. Not just clean from heroin but to live a clean life, to get away from the dirty crack-house living arrangements. You do realize that you're like the only person in Hamilton that's not a gentry homesteader and is also not an addict?

Most of the young whites moving in are coming for the drugs. Baltimore is flush, with [China] white, with rock [crack], with kick [cocaine-fortified heroin] and more oxys than you can imagine. But where the drugs are is where the rehab is—up east here. Florida is nice but it's a one-way ticket. Up here you can go both ways. I know that people say rehab is a cult and a place to buy pills, everybody chain-smoking, still around the same drug mentality—that is true. But I need the support.

I'm going to do this, Sir, going to beat the system, going to live clean in every way. Have a blessed day and thanks for listening.

I am pleased to inform the reader that Cecil does not yet—and hopefully will never—have the hollow, soulless voice of the lifetime heroin addict, which seems to fix sometime in the late 20s.

The Nods

At the End of Time After Party

Readers have asked me why the 40% of Baltimore that is Caucasian does not seem willing or able to combat the aggression of the Harm City goon squads that prowl the streets of the urban wasteland and the suburban promised land.

I went out today and interviewed Cecil, a recovering heroin addict, which you may find in the next chapter. The problem is Caucasians in Baltimore are doing one of three things:

1. Working their ass off as individuals in the fractured social matrix that is designed to make lone victims of us all.

2. Cowering in fear from their brawny and youthful oppressors, having been conditions since babyhood to hold blacks as super athletes and depend on the police for protection, most whites are peculiarly incapable on a physical or psychological level, of defending themselves against the people that the former conservative matrix declared owned all things physical. Not familiar with black urban culture, must whites do not realize that most black men are mental basket cases who dry at the drop of a hat and are as physically effeminate as their white counterparts, playing the same video games and raised according to a louder, ruder version of the same feminist ethos.

3. They are dissipating according to their class: playing video games, enjoying fine dining and microbrew beer, getting immersed in porn, joining swingers clubs or doing drugs in their many varieties, foremost among them heroin, the ultimate black lotus of apathy. There are so many heroin addicts in Baltimore that two in every ten white adults over 30 has that hollow dead tone to

their voice that is the life time mark of heroin.

The Nods

The Nods are the street name of a local Hamilton family of paleface Caucasoidal apes of the inferior type.

Mother Nod is a heroin addict of about 40, who looks 60 and leads her brood around in a drooling clutch behind her leathery mask of dissipation. She uses her food stamps to buy sodas and doughnuts.

Brother Nod is 21, like his mother, a smack head, drooling, nodding, and using his EBT card to cash in at 50-cents on the dollar at the grocery store for money to buy is drugs.

Sister-in-law Nod, is Brother Nod's girlfriend, who came into town from posh Harford County to life the heroin life and spends Moneygram transfers from her parents to keep the needle hot.

Sister Nod is 15, and has been a heroin addict since 12, trained by her mother in the art of scrounging for smack, smoking discarded cigarette butts, blowing Mexican construction workers for quarters, etc.

Today, as I stood outside of the Pakistani liquor store counting my money they all four stood before me drooling and nodding, their four brains seemingly linked in a telepathic attempt to conclude if it could be taken. I started at them and they all four shook as if they were one plant like organism recoiling from a weed whacker and staggered along out of y way.

If I were king I'd use them to grease the CSX railway.

'Fifty Sticks'

The Truth About The Race War

An excellent aspect of Molyneux's treatment here is the pointing out that character references of the person the media sides with are sought and the person who the media sides against is utterly alienated, with the media not seeking character references for the person being lynched in the media. Stefan's usual attention to detail, works very well in this study of how the media uses its influence to form an emotive response from the population and move the enraged population to acts of violence or compliance.

This is not just a recap of the resent race cases in the media. Stefan goes into the history of American Government interest pitting whites and blacks against each other, particularly the mature form of American chattel slavery which held blacks in bondage and forced poor whites to act as unpaid slave-catching police at the same time that the very existence of slavery drove down the price of labor and kept most whites poor.

The fact that communism killed more than 11 times as many people inside of Russia than the Nazis killed Jews during WWII kind of puts the former Soviet menace into perspective. Of interest, along these lines, is the fact that Nazis recruited black soldiers during WWII by using photos of whites attacking blacks in U.S. riots.

I love the KBG agents posing as KKK members and Al Sharpton's protection racket! There is a lot of dystopian nerd fodder here. Enjoy.

Stefan's closing message here is probably his best in recent years and it won't get through. Still, it was well-delivered.

https://www.youtube.com/watch?v=qfcDIw ky8lU

'The First White Construction Worker'

Thomas Sowell - Fallacies of Race, The Tragic Vision of Life and the Growing Roles of Intellectuals in Public Life

© 2016 James LaFond

Blacks had lower unemployment than whites in 1890 and 1930?

Whites had a hard time getting into construction work in the south?

Throughout these interviews, Sowell repeatedly refers to the U.S. as a democracy, which will turn most viewers off. And yes, the U.S, is officially a republic. But Sowell knows that America has gone the way of Athens and is, in effect, a democracy managed by demagogues.

The second link is gold and exposes the racism of progressive liberalism. Thomas Sowell is a good scholar, a fair writer and the only dude in America allowed to speak the truth, so he is a man well worth listening to. His best talks were with fellow black conservative scholar Walter Williams on radio. Hopefully we can find some of these. If you are a racial determinist make sure you go to 13:00 and listen to the IQ study of the children of American Servicemen in West Germany.

The last link explores the "vision of the anointed" versus "the tragic vision" in society and is an examination of intellectual range and the pathology of intellectualism. If the reader wishes to know how deep the rabbit hole is that the American mind has been sucked down, this interview is acutely instructive.

https://www.youtube.com/watch?v=g6IJV_0p64s

https://www.youtube.com/watch?v=9ESlS2jrhXY&ebc=ANyPxKqh2urdbubnzmBHrH_MYfb3kAqU01K7iouaZLW45lo2jqfXmFTNCxsLqLkASONwIyBQQbiHcwX8Rndkm71bIy3V63cufw

https://www.youtube.com/watch?v=Wln6lN
TxVpY&ebc=ANyPxKo_R6ifVv7q1mDyzNHMx
xJxt6vRrSILk-
v9zW0AKnP1t7pZM_ZHAkBra3znZ1GFziZG7
scLO2L_IOVl5EdmIdYMHFayEA

'The Naughtiness of My Heart'

A Profile of an Indigenous Resistance Leader: The Candlelit World of Increase Mather, Part Two of Four

A Brief History of the Warr with the Indians in New-England, Boston, 1676

In his seminal work Increase Mather documented the good and the bad about his society and its native opponents in the war to alter the ecology and sociology of what he called New-England and the New Israel. The book has been reprinted by a white nationalist publisher who placed the following blurb on the back cover:

"This gripping narrative account provides not only an insight into the defensive war which the United Colonies (Massachusetts, Plymouth, and Connecticut) waged against a treacherous enemy who attacked and murdered their settlements without provocation but also of the religious fanaticism which drove the early European pioneers in North America."

Having now read this account three times, in three layers, as it was written, I find the above statement to be grotesquely distorted and untrue, but make no claim that this is intentional. Rather, such a crude reading of this layered and nuanced text, written by a man so passionate about the purity of the truth that he included truths which grossly contradicted his own sacred cause, is to be expected by a modern reader.

I am not a modern reader and have done most of my reading from among ancient sources, which predate the mid 20th century corruption of the written word into a tool of persuasion and obfuscation instead of one of information.

The revolution in advertising writing and of propaganda circa 1930, has resulted in two general types of nonfiction writing: advertising, which includes propaganda, most prominent of which are three-tiered news pieces, and the thesis, including opinion and most books. Both of these types of writing rely on a crude text and a supportive or obliterated subtext intended to support the text. Whereas an honest chronicle such as Mather's provides its own contradictory subtext, the modern reader is conditioned only to read the gross text. Hence, the blurb above is exactly the message that Increase was trying to send down through the ages. But his honest reporting of the facts on the ground sent a concurrent and contradictory echo along with it.

Lastly, the reason for the blurb on this back cover is tied in with postmodern white resistance to the current massive influx of immigrants holding different values and speaking a different language. In profiling "King Phillip" or Metacomet, I will present the case that Increase Mather's book does present an example of an unprovoked attack on natives, but rather than the unsuccessful attack he intended to describe, present a much broader and ultimately successful attack on native peoples supplied by his own subtext.

New England Back-Story

From approximately 1500 through 1620 Basque, Portuguese, Spanish, French, Dutch, Italian and English fisherman, whalers and explorers raided the New England coast for sex slaves and also traded with the stronger coastal tribes, resulting in a 90% die-off of natives via introduced disease, which emptied the coast for English, Swedish and Dutch settlement.

Once settled on the coast, and possessing useful tools, the English of the 1620s were peacefully engaged by the inland natives of the piedmont or hilly regions.

By the late 1630s, increased immigration, disease, habitat destruction and drug addiction introduced by the English and Dutch drove a resistance movement by the natives which was crushed with firearms and by alliances with the Mountain tribes such as the cannibal Mohawks.

By the 1660s, the natives were suffering from all the above ills, and were now sharing their land with a booming English population fed by massive immigration. The English were now also natives, and regarded the resulting conquest of the tribes as the ancient peaceful order of things. The weak English plantation governments did give firearms to allied and compliant subject tribes and banned firearm ownership among tribes that resented the destruction of their ecology. In the English case, it must be said that the government, such as it was, did decree against alcohol sale to young Indians and even stipulated that English livestock must be fenced in to prevent trampling of native habitat.

However, tanneries ruined fishing waters, English pirates kidnapped Indian women and children, Dutch traders addicted young Indian men to rum, English merchants cheated Indian women in trade and many escaped English white slaves joined the Indians and told them of the English long term plan, which was to convert to Christianity or eliminate native peoples.

All of these things were alluded to or plainly stated by Mather, and he did decree that the Indians had been wronged by the English, making his only case for defense the fact that "the government was innocent." In other words, the government was only ultimately responsible for protecting whites from Indians and not doing direct harm to Indians, but not protecting Indians [who they barred from armament] from whites.

In supplements to the narrative Increase Mather exposes the treaty fraud perpetrated upon Metacomet and his handful of allies. Below is a quote from a treaty that Metacomet was made to sign in 1671, when it was ruled that his non-compliance with English wishes would result in him paying punitive fines:

"Whereas my Father, my Brother and my self have formerly *submitted our selves and our people unto the Kings Majesty of England, and to this Colony of New-Plymouth,* by solemn Covenant under our hand; but I having of late through my indiscretion, and the naughtiness of my heart violated and broken this my Covenant with my friends by *taking up Armes [1]*, with evil intent..."

Is there any doubt in the reader's mind that Metacomet did not compose the above admission of guilt?

The publisher of this book did not read the declaration of "submission" by the Indians to an international order as a war condition and then goes along with Increase's contention that the Indians were not conquered people but willing wards of the State, despite his own voluminous testament to the contrary.

The greatest omission by the modern publisher is that the account is made to look like an Indian versus English war of offense, when it was an Indian versus English and Indian uprising by a conquered people, who were utterly doomed and had zero prospect of victory.

The Rival Alliances

The following is taken from the account of Increase Mather, and supplemented by a reading of T. H. Breen's Puritans and Adventurers.

The rebel tribes under Metacomet fielded a force of about 1,000 fighting men, and lost a total of about 2,000 killed, resulting in absolute genocide, leaving less than 1,000 noncombatants and POWs to be sold into slavery or executed. To put this in perspective, the population of Boston had as many white and black servants as the entire allied Indian population.

Metacomet's warriors were drawn from the following tribes, and included a handful of escaped white servants, one of which was publicly executed after capture:

1. Wompanoag [or Mount Hope Indians], Metacomet's tribe

2. Pocasset, led by a female chief

3. Narragansets

4. Nipmuck

5. River Indians

The English-Indian Alliance:

1. Soldiers of Plymouth [hundreds]

2. Soldiers of Massachusetts [hundreds]

3. Soldiers of Connecticut [hundreds]

4. Praying Indians [hundreds, from all three colonies]

5. Volunteers from Rhode island [less than a hundred]

6. Pequod Indians [less than a hundred]

7. Mohawk Indians [300-plus]

8. Cape Indians [less than a hundred]

9. Nattick Indians [less than a hundred]

10. Pirates! [less than a hundred]

11. Monehegins [hundreds]

12. Armed black servants [under a hundred]

13. Armed white servants [hundreds]

Metacomet was surrounded on all sides, had nowhere to run, was arrayed against a superiorly equipped, fortified foe which outnumbered his warriors at least three to one and included the most effective fighting men, being:

1. English Pirates who would also conduct mop-up operations against the white/black slave uprising in Virginia in the later part of 1676, after Bacon's [3] death in October. This New England war was fought from Sumer 1675-Autumn 1676, with the crushing of Simon's [a Metacomet imitator] resistance, with the Cavalier Governor of Virginia wishing the Indians well against the Puritans.

2. Captain Church's mixed Indian/Indian hunter recon force

3. The Mohawks, who were a match for Metacomet's forces on their own, and who

exterminated most of the Wompanoag women and children and elders.

When Metacomet failed to trick the Mohawk enemy into an alliance against the whites he was doomed, but fought on in any case, with Increase Mather wondering out loud at the pain the chief must have felt at the loss of his people and his only child, for the English out-bred the Indians by a 5-1 rate and routinely beat their children, finding it quite odd that, "...the Indians are marvellous fond and affectionate toward their Children..."

The Comparative Case

Metacomet found himself in the following position:

1. The chiefs of his father's generation invited strangers to come and share their land.

2. The strangers bore far more children than the natives.

3. The majority of the inhabitants—both native and stranger—agreed that his people

should give more to the common good than the newcomers.

4. The traditional right of a warrior to go about armed was taken away by common agreement, giving the far more numerous newcomers a great advantage.

5. Men of a criminal sort from among the newcomers began molesting the women and children of the people.

6. Everywhere he turned the face of the land was being altered to accommodate dwellings for newcomers.

7. Natives who defended themselves against newcomers were punished by the government but newcomers who harmed natives were not so punished.

8. The religion and codes of behavior that had once held sway and under which he had been raised, were now objects of ridicule and derision, while the new values of those people protected by the government were port fourth as the basis for social intercourse.

9. Agreements were made in a language that was only clearly understood by the officials of the government which was partial to the newcomers.

10. The newcomers were of various races and spoke multiple languages yet held to a common international ethos.

11. The government seemed to favor the rude people who crowded together in the great towns and everywhere a free man looked, he was surrounded by enemies, either by traitors, traditional foes or newcomers hostile to his way of life.

What was such a beleaguered man to do other than fight or go quietly into the night?

Now, decide for yourself, who more shared the plight of modern palefaces in regards to the government and their neighbors, the Puritans and their Indian subjects, Indian allies, black servants, white servants and military contractors, or Metacomet and his Indian allies?

Notes

1. In 1671 Metacomet was found guilty of procuring guns for his warriors, either for defense against the gun-armed Mohawk enemy [cannibal allies of the English] or for the cause of throwing off the yoke of English conquest, not of actually attacking English settlements or persons.

2. Metacomet was slain by one of Church's Indian scouts.

3. Bacon was the white rebel leader of the mixed white/black slave force that bested the mixed white/Indian/back/pirate slave master army in Virginia but then died of dysentery soon after burning Jamestown to the ground.

'Knowledge Weighs Nothing'

STW Episode #14 – Mike Lummio on Bushcraft

Jack Donovan has really been upping his STW schedule and, with this podcast, has gotten completely out of the meathead zone with a science-based approach to interacting with nature.

Mark Lummio is such a commonsense man it is refreshing, particularly his tool-kit doctrine. The tool segment should be listened to a couple of times. The tarp-based campsite is what I always used back when I was a young guy getting out of the city, and back then I relied on an Australian-based Bushcraft book that didn't address American vegetation. Mark's examination of Modern Western man's antagonist relationship with nature being rooted in Near Eastern desert theology was equally refreshing.

Check out Mark at the link below.

http://www.jack-donovan.com/axis/2016/04/stw-episode-14-mike-lummio-on-bushcraft/

'Maya'

Zero Dark Thirty: The Award Winning Film

I recall reading a memoir by one of the Navy SEALs that killed Osama Bin Laden concerning the substance of this movie. He was dismissive of the Hollywood depiction of the operation, but did say that the move accurately portrayed the CIA bitch-spook who led the quest to find and kill the architect of the 911 attacks with a rabid intensity.

The acting was all excellent. And the tension among operators was effectively maintained throughout the film. How accurate this movie was, I cannot know. I can tell you that it is not a jingoistic glorification of the secular crusade against Militant Islam. There are no 'good guys' in this film. The Islamists and the CIA people are all portrayed as evil obsession personified to such an extent that all acts are justified.

There is one scene where two female analysts, who believe they have set up a meeting with Osama Bin Laden's doctor, talk the CIA paramilitaries into letting the subject drive through the gate and up to a group of seven CIA persons. The lead analyst is gleeful about the prospect that her geek internet search and viewing of brutal interrogations will soon result in bagging Bin Laden. Of course, the car is packed with C-4 and they are all turned into a shit stain in the desert. This scene still grips and disgusts me and also serves as a moral compass for this war, which is just getting under way, a war between girls and boys sitting behind computer screens and sending robots and super-soldiers out to kill, while the priests of the far more ancient materialistic cult they oppose send out their flesh-bots with bombs strapped to them in a brutal medieval parody of an airstrike.

Zero Dark Thirty does not, like Olympus Has Fallen, heroize torturers. Instead it paints a picture of two evil entities hunting each other's meatpuppets across a largely neutral meatscape from the varied isolation of their medieval dungeons and capitalist towers.

While billed as the celebration of the "greatest manhunt in history," I see Zero Dark Thirty's sympathy for little CIA Maya, tear-streaked, brat-smirking angel of death to be the overture for a hundred years of soulless religious war, a century-long duel between the remote mass murderers of the feminists and patriarchs maniacally committed to advancing their competing globalist ideals.

It's worth a view.

http://www.bing.com/search?q=sero+dark+thirty+trailer&form=CPDTDF&pc=EUPP_CPDTDF&src=IE-SearchBox

'Grinning Like a Fool'

One Paleface's Strategy For Surviving Harm City

A reader named SidVic, who has a real job and cannot write stuff like this under his Government name in the looming shadow of Mother Correct, has left such a good comment on an evasion piece that it simply must be posted as an article.

I took a position at U of M School of Medicine in 1996. I worked on Greene Street. I was in Japan at the time I accepted the position and they sent me an orientation packet. I digress, but my background is strict Scot-Irish southern. Anyways the advice for Baltimore, in this UM packet, was as follows: wear comfortable running shoes, don't carry items, keep hands free, walk close to street not buildings, telephones with direct access to security are on every block (plus they assured that if you were incapacitated that it was just necessary to get the phone out of the cradle and the cavalry would arrive!) etc etc....

I was robust young and remember laughing it off. My Jap friends were genuinely shocked and concerned. Back then I regularly re-grew appendages when they had gotten broken off....

Anyways, despite being a complete idiot I seldom ventured into the red zone of your map (good work on the map by the way). I did eat and park north of the market (found cheap roof lot), however. So I found occasion to travel in the red zone, sometime late. A couple of times I was very alarmed among a large group of youngish black males, but I never had any serious problems. I made eye contact and smiled broadly at all. I was surprised that northern negroes seemed surly compared to those I was used to in the south (not all—some were sweet as hell).

I remember telling a black Baltimore friend (he was West Indies originally—they are good people) who was quizzing me on how I found Baltimore about my strategy of grinning like a fool. He laughed uproariously and told me to keep with what was working.

In retrospect, I believe that I was lucky mostly, and that my smiley demeanor was unusual enough to keep them off me.

SidVic, thank you. It is my opinion that your strategy worked because the hoodrats thought you were insane! According to noted African American scholar T. Spoone Slickens, "One of the most common phobias among blacks is fear of retarded white folks."

'Give it Up, Yo'

Black Spring Survival Guide #6

April, 2016, Middle River, Baltimore County

Out on the Redneck Waterfront, where I work, where real white men still walk the streets in defiance of Black Supremacy, Bill was walking home from work at about Ten on a weekday night, at the true end of the welfare month, when the welfare mammies send their young bucks out looking for white folks to rob. On the secondary street of Orems Road a car with two black dudes pulled up next to the sidewalk on which Bill was walking. The two guys bailed out and demand that Bill hand over his money. Never having worked for a living, or having known an employed person, these two idiots did not realize that it was Thursday night and Bill didn't have shit on him. But he fought anyway, fought the two bucks to stand a still, until another car with two more black thugs in it rolled up and joined the fight against their evil oppressor.

Unlikely to prevail against four guys at once, Bill stood his ground on the sidewalk and began yelling for help in this white residential area, unfortunately still inhabited by real white men who do not appreciate the government moving gangs of predators into nearby Essex to prey upon them. Soon porch lights came on, doors began opening, and the sissy Negroes fled the scene without Bill's paltry end-of-the-week cash.

What Should a Paleface do in Bill's Situation?

Do what Bill did!

I might suggest picking up garden bricks when a car rolls up and launching one through the windshield and maintaining the other to cave in a yammering coconut. The cops might come after you for the damage to the car but it will help prevent these sissies from driving off effectively when your neighbors get on the scene. This is a neighborhood invasion and should be treated like one.

Fuck the police!

'White Giants?'

Tara MacIsaac on Native American Myths of Ancient White Giants at Ancient Origins

First, thank you, Ishmael for this link.

Secondly, I really dislike these media heavy commercial sites that beat up my computer and slow it for writing, posting and publishing. It's a shame that I won't search this site as it bogs down my low-powered unit.

The concept of indigenous whites in North American is exciting and currently taboo in most quarters. It used to be the province of strict diffusionist thinkers who believed that every one of man's invention, even the most simple, was unique and was propagated by cultural contact. This obviously meant that ancient Egyptians were advising the Mayans, etc. I for one, think that if you put two stones in front of a primitive man, that he's likely to come up with a similar use for them as some other hunter faced with similar needs on the other side of the globe.

Tara does point out in this article that a battle with fur trappers may account for one such legend. Of course there is a lot of speculation about Vikings going as deep into the continent as the Detroit area.

For those interested in one well done fictional treatment that took plausible turns whenever possible, check out James Alexander Thom's Children of First Man, about how a Welsh Prince fled medieval Britain and established a colony on the Gulf Coast, which migrated up the Alabama watershed and then down the Cumberland watershed to the Missouri to become the Mandan, who, according to painter George Gatlin, claimed to have had white ancestors.

http://www.ancient-origins.net/myths-legends/ancient-race-white-giants-described-native-legends-many-tribes-005774

'A Sobering Report'

90% of 13-Year-Olds at Italian School Would Convert to Islam if ISIS Came to Their Home

© 2016 James LaFond

Thanks to Deuce for this link.

If you are interested in Islamic encroachment in Europe and the U.S. Robert Spencer at Jihad Watch seems to have the most comprehensive data pool and also knows how to interpret the information.

Personally I have long been of the opinion that though Charles Martel may have stopped the scimitars of the Crescent from sweeping through Europe, that his descendent, Charlemagne set up Europe for eventual Islamic conquest when he successfully spread Christianity at the point of a sword. Over the world, Pagans and heathens in Indian, Africa and Asia have proved more resistant to the seduction of Islam than Christians. The Vikings were fierce opponents of Islam. But, the adoption of so many pagan deities into the cult of the Catholic saints [look at our days of the week: Moonday, Thor's Day, Freya's Day, Saturn's Day, Sunday] made Cathlocism palatable enough for pagans for the power hungry rulers to win conversions to the submissive Christian way. Christianity, looked at this way, is the way station between paganism and Islam.

In my mind, if anything truly doomed Christianity to fall before Islam it was the Reformation, which largely scrubbed pagan elements from the religion and hastened the secularization of Christianized Europeans. This may seem nutty and I am a renowned crackpot. But when you borrow a desert religion and sell it in a forested land by mixing in the local beliefs, and then scrub the local beliefs out, the faith that is left will be vulnerable to a competing faith born in the desert and true to itself. Hell, during the Turkish conquest of Europe they were only resisted by Catholics and Greek orthodox

Christians. While the Polish cavalry was rescuing their fellow Austrian Catholics, the English navy would not even protect its home waters from Turkish slave raiders!

Where I see Islam failing to prevail is in Eastern Europe, catholic Latin America, and in those portions of America where Protestantism has taken on charismatic forms and folkways. Catholicism in its American version is dying like a lich in his tomb, and mainstream Protestantism in America has become too secularized to survive commercialism let alone Islam. I predict, that within 90 years, those portions of North America that have not been colonized by Latinos or maintained by Christian fundamentalists will be ruled by an American caliphate.

Savor the character of some emerging youth via the link below.

https://www.jihadwatch.org/2016/04/robert-spencer-in-frontpage-90-of-13-year-olds-at-italian-school-would-convert-to-islam-if-isis-came-to-their-home

'Make Room, Make Room!'

U.S. Suicide Rate Surges to a 30-Year High

© 2016 James LaFond

A friend's next door neighbor killed himself a few months ago.

I know three people whose parents killed themselves.

My favorite author killed himself.

And apparently it is getting worse.

Some interesting aspects here will let us track social change.

White women, the very people that have done the most to dismantle Western Civilization over the past century, are finally beginning to increase the rate at which they off themselves similar to the tormented men they have been driving to suicide since World War I. They do have some ground to make up, though. So it will be a while before we see parity in actual numbers.

The only group of people who are killing themselves less frequently is black men. But that is more than made up for by the fact that black men are so selflessly willing to relive their fellows of the horrors of human suffering that suicide has become obsolete!

Overall, however, despite the fact that the black dudes are slacking off, the overall U.S. suicide rate is surging ahead.

How do you say, "Make room, make room!" in Spanish?

Joy, joy, joy!

http://www.amren.com/news/2016/04/u-s-suicide-rate-surges-to-a-30-year-high/

About the Title

The Harry Harrison novel, Make room, Make room! was made into the movie Soyient Green starring Charlton Heston.

https://www.youtube.com/watch?v=LozJSTjrvek

Shane and Odin

A Man and His Dog Stand Against Evil as Night Falls on the Western World

© 2016 James LaFond

As I make my way around Harm City on foot I make the odd acquaintance. The most complex of these are human-canine pairings.

There is Penny the doll baby beagle and her bearded hipster master, ripened wheat awaiting the hoodrat sickle.

There is Joe the boxer who keeps mistaking me for his master as his co-owner—a cougar named Ellen—assures me that I must be a good person if Joe think I'm his master.

There is May, the border collie whose redheaded human guide will someday soon be attacked by my enemies as she politely wanders side streets at night where I no longer go unarmed.

There is Russell, the big hairy mutt who belongs to John, a black fellow of about my age who marches about deliberately with his 80-pound dog carrying a large oak stave, knowing that the vile spawn of his younger "brothers" will one day attack him for his dog in hopes of feeding it to a pit-bull.

John and I know that the young thugs of Harm City have and will attack us under police sanction and that we are on our own. The rest are clueless, potentially-suffering meat for the ever-turning psychological spit of Black Spring, of the secret race war against palefaces being launched in plain view as the media, government and cops look the other way.

I just met another man, walking his dog on my street, who has altered his route due to a recent incident and was inquiring of me as to the thug matrix, virulence of the hoodrat infestation, etc., just this morning as I took out the trash.

His name is Shane, a Vietnam Combat Veteran who served one tour with a unit one of my step-brothers served with. He wanted his unit obscured along with his name. Shane's dog is a 120-pound German police dog named Odin, who is a good boy and nuzzled me after I petted him.

A few days ago Shane was walking Odin late in the afternoon when three bike-boys [14-16-year-old blacks who work for drug gangs as scouts, spotting cops, likely robbery and burglary targets, and—at two a week in Hamilton—seize dogs for use as pitbull bait.] These patrols wax numerous and aggressive at the end of the month, now concentrating their activity between the 26th and 30th. This incident happened on the 29th, at the very time when hoodrat mammas send their spawn out to pillage and rob on their behalf.

The three hoodrats stopped peddling lazily in the middle of the street and the leader walked his bike toward Shane as Odin stood ready beneath him, ready to act. The leader said, "I like that dog, yo. I thinks I needs myself a dog. I thinks this is my dog."

Just as Shane decided that this was it, that he was going to fight these hoodrats to the death right here, rather than hand over the family dog, Odin let out a roaring bark that turned into a slathering snarl, and the hoodrat scampered onto his bike and peddled off with his subhuman fellows.

Shane said, "I'm not backing down from those motherfuckers! This might be the hood now, and I can't afford to move, but I'll fight before I roll over and die. I will walk my dog where I want."

I informed Shane that the usual course in such a situation was for the white owner to get intimidated, confusing his dog and then to let the blacks pet the dog—further confusing the dog and betraying him as well—and then to have the most skilled dog handler among the blacks walk the dog off as the owner abandoned him in the face of verbal threats and assault [threatening posture and crowding.] I warned him about letting his wife walk Odin, unless he is the type of dog that is aggressively territorial, in which case he would probably protect her as she called the cops, who still protect white women on occasion. But even so, she could get knocked around and dragged. Odin also has to learn hatred of blacks, so that he cannot be coaxed out of a yard and into a van.

I hope Odin and Shane never have to make hoodrat contact, otherwise he might end up in Jail and/or prison as his dog is executed by the State. For just last week, a police officer in East Baltimore encountered a thirteen-year-old hoodrat wielding a pellet-pistol which was an authentic nine-millimeter replica and is now facing the inquisition for shooting the little bastard. If the bully goons of the State are persecuted for defending themselves against gun-armed youths, what will happen to a paleface and his dog when the Hoodrat Lives Matter paen goes up over the ruins of a city that was and the evil song of the MediaState takes up the shrill chorus?

'A Journey of the Heart'

The foreword by Karl H. Schlesier to Penucquem Speaks: A Look at Our World from a Different Culture by Ronald Thomas West

© 2016 James LaFond

Mr. Schlesier's foreword to Penucquem Speaks is approximately a 1,300-word essay on alienation using the case of Ronald Thomas West in relation to his adoption by the Blackfeet people as his reference. For any readers disenchanted with our modern materialistic megaculture, this makes insightful reading as Mr. Schlesier breaks the culture into three components in reference to alienation and inclusion. What he refers to as the greater white society is in itself also a disintegrating culture that is suffering the same thing that the Blackfeet suffered at the hands of white, Christian America. This white, Christian America in its various subcontexts is being dismantled for a greater good—the greater good of globalism. Schlesier singles out the greatest threat to a culture as being those people from that culture who assimilate into the greater entity and work toward its dismantling for the good of the greater outside entity. Below is the three-part scheme that Schlesier lays out. To help understand this, when you read Blackfeet, read American; and when you read American, read globalism or liberalism or whatever extra-national ideology or entity you wish.

1. Cultural Entity: "Blackfeet culture today, as it survives on and off the reservation, has lost much of its complexity and splendor of old but still maintains features and behavior patterns and values that are attractive. The Blackfeet people still exist, and many are much like the people as they used to be a long time ago. Today they are often burdened by sets of problems they have no control over."

2. Cultural Orphans: "There are also Blackfeet who are lost, who seem to belong

nowhere, neither to the Blackfeet world nor to the White world."

3. Cultural Traitors: "And there are those who work against their own people for the benefit of surrounding Whites and for local and national schemes to defraud them."

"Of these three groups the first can be assisted, the second must be left to the ceremonial people to heal, and the third group must not only be endured but must be fought."

In this reader's view what Karl Schlesier refers to when he speaks of whites and white society is materialism, for at the point of contact with white Christians, Christianity in its American form was part of an industrial, mercantile sales package—the embedded theology that came with the secular goods. If we look to our own situation as Americans, whatever type we see ourselves as, we see our leaders making decisions to benefit a greater, global good that is forever about increased profit, reduced labor costs, increased centralization, and has only one end, which is the reduction of a human being to an economic unit.

'The Stone War Hammer'

Backdrop to Penucquem Speaks by Ronald Thomas West

In this tribal backstory, Ronald references his primary source – two traditional Blackfeet Indians, Floyd Heavy Runner, War Chief and Medicine Man Pat Kennedy. What follows is a brief overview of the tribal structure which recognizes five branches and two branches which are adopted subtribes from outside of the original tribal line.

The focus of this brief history was the defrauding of the Blackfeet people of their sacred lands by four individuals, one of whom was a traitor chief. He describes the political structure of the tribes as theocratic and republican and makes the point that the US government insisted on viewing the tribe as autocratic. From my reading of the history of American expansion, this was the formula: to pretend that we were dealing with kingdoms rather than tribal confederacies and tribal republics. Such traditional tribal systems are much more stable than the American republican system, based as it was on the ancient Roman system which utterly failed to forestall empire and tyranny.

West refers to an incident in 1855, when a chief named Little Dog gave mapping information to a railroad and was then killed by chiefs enforcing the law. He goes on to relate how in 1895, the Blackfeet chief, Three Suns, "would have visited death by the stone hammer, smashed their skulls, upon White Calf, Joe Kipp, James Willard Schultz, and George Bird Grinnell, as the prime Blackfeet associated players, for the part they played in the theft of Blackfeet lands."

The picture we see painted is of local, tribal law being trumped by federal law that permitted a whiskey trader, an artist, a traitor chief, and an "Ivy League type" rich boy to steal the sacred heart of the land and sell it, with their self-serving, misrepresented claims going down in history as an objective record of events. As someone who was on the ground as the race purge of 2015 swept across the portions of Baltimore that I frequent, now looking back through the media lens which declares that it was a noble uprising, and only a drugstore was burned and a mall looted, it is easy to believe that one hundred years could do even more to obscure the truth in the hands of the same ruling class. If in one year we, as a nation, have come to believe an absolute lie fabricated from whole cloth that is counter to the truth, while those who lived through it still stand and speak in their thousands, how hard is it to imagine that a hundred years could similarly cloak a lie?

'Nice Neighbors'

A Plunge Down the Paleface Eradication Rabbit Hole

This weekend, as I spent time with family in celebration of the put-upon woman who was tasked with bringing me into the world, I did pay attention to the American Narrative as it stands. I simply noted the race and gender of the commercial actors and the groupthink orators as they were presented for my complaisance, as a way of determining what type of people are preferred by my unseen masters. In following the Presidential Race, it seems the only two stories in public discourse today are race and gender, as stated by the future Queen of America as she spoke on the racism and sexism of the False-Haired One.

Below is the tally of speakers by race and gender that came into view on my Mother's

TV this weekend. The programming was 80% local and 20% national, none global, this being the only nation on earth that generates news.

Locally and nationally male and female populations are roughly 50/50.

Nationally black and white population is 6 to 1 white.

I realize we have other races and that Latinos outnumber blacks by at least 2 to 1, but the media assures me otherwise. For certainly, if there were a Latino population of any significance in America there would be representation in TV programming, correct?

Asians? Who are they? The media assures me that there are a few, but that they are firmly aligned and identified with blacks and black causes, so, Cracker, please!

Locally the white and black population is 10 to 2. That is right, a third of Baltimoreans are white and virtually all people in the surrounding counties are white, so it's about 5 to 1.

Experts poled on the Kentucky Derby had whites outnumbering blacks by 3 to 1. Obviously, all of those black millionaires make horse racing the preferred sport, so this is understandable. Also though most of the riders were Latino, not one Latino expert was poled!

The general sports casting jobs were all held by white men at the local level and were dominated by white men at 3 to 2 nationally.

Of local news anchors, half were black men and half were white women. On the local news white men are only trusted with sports, and to a lesser extent, weather.

Self help gurus were 2 black men, 3 white women, 2 black women, 1 Asian woman and 1 white man. 5 to three in terms of gender, no Latinos and slightly tilted favoring whites, but still not in line with viewer proportions.

Admittedly the below is a small sample of perhaps 20 commercials.

The most fascinating aspect was the fact that in all of the many commercials I saw depicting American men as fathers and or mates there was only 1 of perhaps 20 commercials that depicted a white man with a white woman, and this commercial depicted two insane white people throwing stuff all over their lawn, while their two highly professional black neighbors sat with a financial adviser unlike the idiot whites, with the white advisor commenting on the idiocy of the white neighbors.

White fathers were only shown with their children when the mother was not present, and he was always made fun of.

The phone ads showed a white woman with an Asian man.

The other ads showed black men with black women or white women.

The only thing I take from this mix of commercials is that a white man and white women mating is seen by the media as some bizarre occurrence, which should not be depicted lest it be emulated and if it does happen, she better keep her distance lest she go insane like him.

'Twerking on Judgment Day'

Tommy Sotomayor rips and rhymes at the expense of our current cultural icons

As I completed formatting America in Chains last night and cracked open a beer I clicked on Tommy Sotomayor's YouTube channel to see what he was up to.

What are Coons?

How stupid are Dumb Black Bitches?

Why do modern African Americans imitate the wig fetish of chattel slavery era English Aristocrats?

Why are the most common calls of racism in fact indictments of working class whites by elite whites and criminal blacks?

Despite this, how come blacks show no racial solidarity unless attacking middle class and working whites?

Why is slavery seen exclusively as a white on black crime when it was manifestly not?

If you believe in matriarchy, this is what it looks like taken to its logical conclusion in a materialistic society where women place their womb at the service of the highest bidder and masculine action is the most taboo act. Now, Tommy claims all of this seemingly insane African American behavior is stupidity. But might it be otherwise? Might these behaviors, counter to civility and notions of the value of hard work—which is the main value Tommy promotes—be calculated, inculcated blue prints for imposing one's paltry will on the social environment?

Recently someone asked me why young black girls slow down while crossing the street in traffic and give an insolent look, daring the motorist to hit them. The answer is that they are trained to do this by a mother who is hoping they get hit so that she hits the law suit sweepstakes. This may seem overblown. But I have had two different black men, one a coworker, the other a fellow bus patron, describe to me how their mothers coached them as little boys to make certain they were struck by a car in the crosswalk and to remember to "roll on the hood."

In my opinion this stems from our slave-based society, in which whites have traditionally sought the formula for success that would gain them access to the wealth of a slave master as well as the moral freedom denied the slave master, while blacks have tended to imitate the haughty, entitled manner of the slave-master and make the same type of interpersonal calculations made by the moral tyrants of a grotesquely materialistic world.

Many people may assume that gaining the power and wealth of the slave master is preferable to simply acting like an ancient potentate. However, the haughtily applied belief in entitlement, while generally failing to generate the desired material gain, does arm the slave-master imitator with a proper understanding of interpersonal power, and in the long view, has evolved into an alliance between the black criminal class and the white and mixed-race elite at the expense of working whites, who insanely tend to continue believing in the Fantasy of Rights. Some palefaces even believe in racial solidarity, that somehow a powerful white person would side with a poor white person against a black aggressor when the sensible thing for the powerful white at the top of the social pyramid to do is to play the bottom off against the middle, for those at the bottom are his natural allies and those in the middle the threat to his hegemony, the potential usurpers of his apex position, from which any fall would be ruinous.

Andrew Johnson and other escaped white slaves of the early 1800s saw their enemy as being the elite white plantation owners working in accord with their slaves to dispossess the working white man. This is the dynamic that fed the westward expansion of the United States as the descendents of Caucasian slaves moved outward and away from the slave system.

Now, 200 years later, with a wage slavery system in effect and nowhere else left to settle away from it, the working paleface finds himself smashed between numerous forces, a situation which was once described by surviving Native Americans as being "caught between two fires." The postmodern paleface is caught:

-between corrupt law enforcement and black criminals

-between the white-hating media and the Black Lives Matter activists

-between a white elite that can buy all of the medical treatment they need and the unemployed criminal classes whose health care is paid, not at the expense of the white elite, but of the working class

-between the multinational corporations, who own 90 of every 100 dollars and the multinational drug cartels that own every street corner in mid-sized U.S. cities...

The sons and daughters of the last generation of Caucasian chattel slaves feared more than anything that their small homestead would be sandwiched between a plantation house and the slave-shacks that served the will of the slave-master.

What does the post-modern paleface see as he stands before the house of his that is losing value as the white elite in their glittering towers and old style plantation-era government buildings decree that unemployed criminals will be his new neighbors?

Is not the poorer-by-the year postmodern paleface living the nightmare of his forefathers, caught between the twin fires of the rich white elite and their human tools— their moral slaves?

This paleface lives in a city across which poor whites have been hunted relentlessly ever since the authorities decided to let angry blacks pillage without interference just over a year ago. On the two mile stretch of road where I walk to work after exiting the bus, where I once regularly saw police patrolling at night, there has not been a cop sighting in exactly a year and two weeks, and over the past two weeks there have been six attacks by groups of black thugs against working whites—and one working ["traitor-snitch"] black man—and the police still decline to patrol. The extinction hunt is on, directed by the white liberal elite, ignored by the white conservative elite and prosecuted by the race-hounds of The New Slave-Master America and working whites are its prey.

That is how this crackpot sees the American Dream from Ground Zero of the Fall of Western Civilization.

If you would like to see how a dissident African American commentator sees the same sorry scene, click on the link below.

https://www.youtube.com/watch?v=5ur7Dd Ikpe8

'Within the Black and Gray Latitudes'

The International with Clive Owen and Armin Mueller-Stahl

© 2016 James LaFond

This film could be viewed as having a leftist slant, if one does not recall that communism set out to crush the industrialists, not banking, and that all forms of crime—most obviously the operation of the protection rackets known as States or governments—are compatible with international banking. The theme is that the generation of debt is the key to both wealth and power and that justice is merely an illusion to blind the morally functioning masses to the fact that they are merely beasts being farmed by an evolving abstraction manned by a parade of sold souls.

Clive Owen plays an Interpol agent trying to bust a Belgian bank. The bank employs an interesting assassin and also an advisor played by Armin Mueller-Stahl, who owns most of the ten best lines in the movie, some of which are quoted below:

"When the lion kills it is the jackal that profits."

"A man can meet his destiny on the road he took to avoid it."

"...[how to] navigate within the black and gray latitudes."

"Justice is an illusion."

"...[between] you and the man you wanted to be."

The old guy even paraphrases Mark Twain's famous quip that though life did not "make sense" "fiction has to."

The counter-theme of The International is one of heroic redemption which does take a surreal man-pause in a Manhattan setting as hipsters [including potential sexual property and worthless faggots] cringe, cower and whimper during an invigorating blood-letting.

Some of the mechanics of international skullduggery [like the above mentioned shootout] are overdone. However, the morality, dialogue and narrative of the tale are scrupulously true to vile life.

Oh, the Naomi Watts character and her man-wife are inserted to get female asses in theater seats and have no real bearing on the heroic narrative.

https://www.youtube.com/watch?v=ILj3Hla oOCg

'The Perfect Masculine Fights'

The Conflict Bindrune by Jack Donovan

Jack begins this piece with making the point that it's more important to have men, then to try and have only good men and miss the boat completely and end up with a feminized sense of manhood that does not value combat for its own sake. I believe that simply fighting bestows virtue.

He then goes into the artistic mummery of deconstructing the sign I have hated since my youth, the peace sign! This had nothing to do with some 10-year's-old's sense of geopolitics, but simply the fact that the hippie's were my oppressors, the teenagers that picked on us. Now, having acquired a distinct distaste for their rancid philosophy I find that a do-it-yourself pagan tribe out on the Left Coast is turning their sacred symbol upside down.

It's a good day to watch Civilization die.

http://www.jack-donovan.com/axis/2016/05/the-conflict-bindrune/

'I Want My Money Back'

America Goes Away by Fred Reed

It has been a while since I have checked in on my favorite curmudgeon, Fred Reed and it seems he is still getting flak for being a race traitor and moving beyond the sacred feminist hive of global America. However, although Fred plays hurt, I think he is just hurting. Alienation is important to a writer and I am certain that failing to piss off his fellow American spawn would lop one of the mouthy heads from his Muse kelpi.

If you don't have time, or have not read Fred and need a nudge, here is a quote from this recent rant:

"In the country where I grew up, if you woke up and found a naked intruder headed for daughter's bedroom with a Bowie knife and a hard-on, you shot him and arranged to have the rugs cleaned. The sheriff wasn't greatly interested and the county prosecutor didn't see anything to prosecute. The scum floating on the gene pool wasn't a protected species. It wasn't the driving engine of the culture. It was just scum."

Now, there is a good reason for Fred to live outside the U.S. and that is that he, and the rest of us bloggers scan expect no protection as members of the press because we do not qualify as we do not have press credentials issued by certified ass-kissing entities approved by the giant ass of State.

Check out Fred's work. The way he ruffles the written word is a pleasure.

Ishmael, thanks for this link.

https://www.lewrockwell.com/2016/05/fred
-reed/america-goes-away/

'I Collect the Bottles'

Violence and Private Security in South Africa by the Liberal Handwringers at Vice

The Vice reporters are good for going where no mangina has gone before and then commenting like guilt-ridden, self-hating, metrosexual clarions of a dead world. They are the zombies that think they are the living, but they do get good footage.

The security employee who lives in a black ghetto and then sneaks off to protect rich whites—pretending to his neighbors that he is collecting bottles for recycling—is a sympathetic soul. I think that 50 years from now America is going to look something like this. And so long as Americans—like these Vice twerps—choose to believe that violence and oppression never existed prior to the invention of these things by their uniquely evil ancestors, it will thrive. The most blissfully ignorant belief about violence is that it is caused by poverty, when virtually all violent deaths among humans have been ordered by the most powerful princes of men and generally carried out by privileged killers.

Ignorance is a beautiful thing.

Speaking of ignorance, look at the black men in this video, then look at the so-called black men in your community, and try to tell me that they are not mixed-race people. Even children can tell the difference between dark chocolate and a KitKat.

https://www.youtube.com/watch?v=pKGzw8GROf0

To the Talbot Boys

A Paleface Win Against the Liberal Slavocracy

Various liberal—and mostly colored [this is how the filing organization describes itself, as a group of "colored" people] Urban Marylanders, and a national cabal of communists, have attempted to have a monument to the 80 Talbot County Maryland men who died fighting for the Confederacy, removed from the grounds of the Talbot County Courthouse.

This monument was not raised until 1916, as an act of social healing, a way of forgiving local men for fighting on the wrong side of a moral conflict.

The current attempt has failed, and was voted down by County legislators. It will be attempted again. That is how wars are fought.

Keep in mind that this is not just a race war on behalf of the new black elite at the expense of the old white majority, which must be systematically reduced to a moral underclass in order to assure that the globalization goals of the international bankers that traffic in national guilt, will never be threatened by nationalistic sentiments among the slaves of the wealthiest fief in the global portfolio.

Masculinity is under assault. The extreme masculinity of these men—who, unlike their sissy, bitch-raised, colored detractors—were so confident in their own manhood that they called themselves "boys," where a bitch-raised colored fellow cannot tolerate the moniker.

The reason given for the leveling of the monument was that these 80 men died to keep blacks in bondage. I agree that they died for this purpose and were misguided in their choice of allegiance. But they paid the ultimate price—the man's price—but the liberal mind will not rest until their ghosts pay the woman's price, erasure of identity.

The most unjust war in American history was surely Vietnam, in which over a million innocent people a world away were slaughtered to satisfy an elitist American fantasy, a war fought on false pretext, a war that ruined the minds of over a million American men and which ripped the guts out of the greatest nation in the world.

The U.S. dropped more ordinance on Vietnam that it did on Nazi Germany and Imperial Japan combined. The war has become a by-word for a dirty war, a miss use of military power that is as damaging to the victor as the loser.

Should we tear down the Vietnam War Memorial?

When nations go to war they *always* go to war for evil purposes and drag armies of doomed souls with them by hook or by crook. If this practice of erasing war dead monuments of the Civil War meets with success it is the first step in a long, morally grueling Hive mind evolution progress, which will completely absolve Governments from the crime of war, and lay the burden instead on its victims.

White slavery was denied by a white-run government for 160 years in order to inculcate the idea that governments did not enslave people, but rather that individuals of certain types did at the expense of other certain types, and government must therefore be all powerful to prevent this— when in fact the truth was that slavery was a government program, welfare for the rich, that was eventually blamed on the poor who did not profit from it and who died in large numbers sorting it out. Likewise, now that war can be blamed on the soldiers, The State might be absolved of evildoing, and citizens of the future global Hive will cheer as machines are used to hunt down warriors, and the warriors are blamed for the ultimate crime, for being human, and worst of all, for being a man, the form of humanity most unacceptable to the Hive.

The Talbot Boys yet stand.

'Boy?'

A Man Question from Eddie Concerning the Etymology of Black America's Most Taboo Word

© 2016 James LaFond

A fellow grocer, upon reading the article about the Talbot County Boys [Maryland Confederates who died in the Civil War], had the following comment:

"I understand a man getting pissed when someone calls him a boy. But last week I had this foodstamper, a nice lady—whose boy, who could have only been four and she had shopping with her at two in the morning—who went ballistic when I returned his toy and said, 'Miss, your boy dropped this.' She went insane, her face pinched up and told me, 'Don' you dare call my little man a boy—that's racist!' Since you're the honorary

African American, I thought maybe you could explain this to me."

-Eddie

We didn't have time to discuss it, so I'm posting it here and will hopefully earn Eddie's readership after he checks it out.

In Black America women often call each other girls in an endearing fashion which has morphed into girlfriend [my mother's generation of white women where still referring to each other as girls a few years ago, although no longer], and men chaff and rage at the term boy, and take every possible opportunity to use the term boy to designate a white man. As a store manager I had numerous parents of child shoplifters who insisted on me referring to their children as a child [chyle] or "little man," with boy, girl or kid unacceptable.

There are news real films extant in which FDR socializes with working men and refers to them as boys, and they have no problem with this. However, these were proud white men, who had been raised by men, where today's black man was raised by a woman who is usually stupid, often insane and always violent, resulting in a high level of emasculation and therefore sensitivity to male imagery—hence rap music, singing about the size of your dick all day long, and the atrociously poor sportsmanship of black professional athletes compared to other groups. This feeling is made worse by the fact that American blacks have been taught that they are the only human beings that have ever been held in bondage other than the Israelites in Egypt.

Ironically, the sensuous pleasure black men and boys—who insist they are men while still in diapers, and hence hopelessly degrading the designation—take in referring to white males their own age as whiteboys [not even with a dash, but one word] while they themselves insist on being referred to as men, is not displaced and is indeed historically correct.

The first slaves referred to as boys in North America were white, and they were referred to as boys, because they were. Child slaves known as "Duty Boys" were being shipped to

America as early as 1621, and had been preceded by just plain old "boys" since 1609, 10 years before the first black slave was shipped to Virginia. For the next 150 years most American slaves were white, and most were trafficked into bondage as children between the ages of 8 and 14, and were accurately called boys and girls.

However, calling a man who has grown to adulthood in chains that you have placed upon his wrists and ankles, a boy, is a psychic blow, and many of these white slaves rebelled and escaped before their indentures were up, earning white American poor the everlasting hatred of the white American elite, who gradually replaced their white slaves with blacks, at great expense, between 1700 and 1800.

The habit of calling slaves boys and girls continued from this child slavery practice that literally birthed this nation and not without reason. For many black slaves on a plantation were the children of the slave master and his male associates, to whom he would pimp his slave women out to for breeding. The white slave master was the father figure of the entire obscene household. To this day many Black Americans refer to the government as White Daddy, and since the black man who has been cast aside by the legions of black women who have married the government in his stead, continues to chaff at the daisy chains of emasculation, the simple word, worn by over 100,000 white boys who were murdered and worked to death clearing the forests of the Eastern Seaboard, is only remembered as a bondage brand by the one and only ethnic group of Americans who failed to win their own freedom, and a century and a half after having it given to them, have decided they don't want it, asking only that such semantic reminders of their position as the moral chattel of an evil state be omitted from discourse, a pathetic demand I have always honored out of pure pity.

'Find Me An American'

Speaking with DSD Dave about Immigrant Labor

Dave is a vendor who services supermarkets, whom I sometimes speak to on my lunch break at about 3 in the morning while he comes in to write his order. I asked him how the remodeling on his house was going and he launched into a tirade:

"Suffice it to say that I am absolutely solid on the Trump candidacy. It's gotten to the point where I just want to live in an English-speaking country. I moved so far out into the fucking country that if I go any farther I'll be living in Philthadelphia and I still can't get away from it. The light fixtures come damaged, so my wife writes a note ascertaining that the damage was on the manufacturer's end and the fucking haji motherfucker who is supposed to do the install cannot understand English well enough to grasp this and he's flipping out thinking that she's trying to get him in trouble.

"I do have a white man I hired to paint the place but he shows up two hours late and leaves two hours early and fucking brings Mexicans with him who can't understand a word I say. So, yesterday, the guy who I contracted with for the blinds has not called me in a week and I'm wondering where him or his people are. I call him and as I'm having the discussion as to why the fuck he can't get someone to install the blinds I reiterate the fact that I want an American to install them, someone I can speak to, who will understand, who gives a shit! And you know what this motherfucker says, he says, 'Find me an American that will work and I'll hire him.' Well, I told him that Americans want to work for a good wage, not what he's paying these people."

As Dave said this he pointed with his head at our Brazilian floor tech, the hardest working guy in the building, so it was time for me to burst his patriotic bubble—which was kind of shitty of me, being that he is the kind of guy that picks up the tab for men in uniform seated near him at a restaurant.

"Dave, that guy makes more money than anyone in the building, overnight, except for you. I used to manage one of these places. I've signed the work orders, have negotiated with contractors and have coached some of these immigrant floor techs. That guy probably costs the owners eighteen-hundred a week and he gets six of that, which is twice what these full-timers get paid and three times what I get paid. The last white American to do floors in Baltimore for a wage was Danny, back in ninety-two. In ninety-two it was a fifteen-an-hour job when union clerks made eleven-forty-an-hour. For a year black guys tried it and they all quit, didn't even stay on as operators because the work is too hard. Now Rick, the guy that worked out how you do floors economically with this equipment, was white—a racist white dude I screwed out of a contract for picking fights with my black janitor—but since ninety-two everyone using his method in Maryland has been an alien. The Eastern Europeans, mostly guys that owned construction and trucking businesses in their home countries in the late eighties, cashed out and moved over here and were doing floors. But they got into construction and trucking as soon as possible and handed it off to Peruvians and Brazilians who primarily run Salvadoran and Mexican workers."

"If the money's good, why won't Americans do floors?" he said with his hands out and his eyes wide and mouth open.

"Look, Dave, it is not any harder than what we do, but is demeaning. Look at the want ads, its all wait staff positions. Americans are too vested in not doing menial work to be a bartender or waiter, even tough those people make good money. The guy that ran USA Boxing in Maryland did it from behind a bar—made three-hundred a night, easy, because he had your drink there for you the way you want it just before you asked. That's how he made his bread. But his masculinity was asserted as an athletic official, a guy checking the tape on a fighter's hands, saving them from going to the hospital by stopping a one-sided beating. That dude was unusual. I had a business professor tell me to drop landscaping and drain digging from my resume because it would portray my character in a negative light. In our culture the man who works, sweats or bleeds is a pariah. Since America is about dollars and nothing else most people look for their identity in their work and they don't want to be the guy pushing the broom because, back in the day, that guy was a slave: property, and most white and black Americans are descended from slaves."

Dave pointed to his own chest and raised his eye brows, "Me, you're trying to tell me that my ancestors that came to this country were fucking slaves?"

"No, Dave, they were Irish so they were not allowed to fuck. Only black slaves could have sex. If your Pennsylvania Irish forefather got caught dipping his wick he'd get seven years tacked on to his indenture. But yes, he was almost certainly a slave."

"Then who the fuck owned him?"

"A liberal, Dave. And if it was in Pennsylvania he was probably owned by a Quaker who was agitating for the freedom of blacks even as he paid Indians to keep the Irish savages on the plantation."

Dave started, and then turned in a huff as he went to his truck, snarking, "I guess not a fucking thing has changed!"

If you would like James to come to your church and give a motivational speech on patriotism and Christian Identity, contact him at jameslafond.com@gmail.com.

'The Ancient Poems of Our Forefathers'

Greg Johnson interviews the legendary hacker and internet troll Andrew "Weev" Auernheimer

"Maybe you could move to this country."

-Mescaline Franklin

As a person who is not a 'racialist' I find racially aligned people to be refreshingly real and enjoy my contact with them, even when they are trying to kill me. As an alien to all races, who happens to look like one of you despicable white apes, it does sometimes vex me that it is expected of non-Caucasian people to be racialists but that you savage whites are not, obviously, to be trusted with racialist sentiments.

One thing I do disagree with white nationalists about is the idea that the plan of elite whites to kill and enslave and breed out poor whites is recent. A friend recently asked me why whites do not stick together.

First, none of the general racial groups stick together, at all: the Chinese are oppressing 11 Asian racial groups, blacks—who have more genetic diversity than the rest of humanity combined—do not seem to be able to kill each other fast enough, brown-on-brown killing is the most prolific form of human killing right now, Cappoid women are still beating their scrawny husbands as they teeter toward extinction and Australoid's in New Guinea and Australia stab their women in the vagina with burning sticks...

As for whites, leaving the Berbers, Semites, Alpines and workhorse Slavs out of it and just looking at the Nords, why have American whites of the economically dominant English strain never stick together?

From 1066 to 1450 the ruling class in England [hold your breath big guy] **spoke**

French and the servile classes spoke Old English. The only reason why the Norman lords began speaking English was because they finally lost their French lands and had to be able to speak to their second tier Anglo-Saxon servants as opposed to just beating and killing them. Even as the language took a unified form—almost immediately, in fact—poverty, homelessness and unemployment were outlawed to facilitate the rulers, gradually taking all of the rest of the land from the common people. The next step was to export these dispossessed lowlifes overseas, to plant them in plantations, and have them enrich the rich as they starved and died. Eventually, these poor English failed to survive in large enough numbers and were replaced with Scotts and Irish, who were such savages they could not be kept on the plantation and actually defeated the aboriginal security forces and broke out. From that moment blacks were shipped in to replace these nasty whites.

So, there was never a time when elite whites in America did not use other whites or other races to oppress their lesser countrymen.

Nothing has changed, and as complicit as certain Hebrews might be in the demise of Western Society, if you removed every one of them nothing would change. The machine is in motion. Changing out gears at this point is like rearranging the deck chairs on the titanic.

http://www.counter-currents.com/2016/04/counter-currents-radio-interview-with-weev/

'Palpable Longing or Instinctive Rage'

Why Whitegenocide Doesn't Work by Vox Day

The emasculation of the political Left is a given. The most comic thing about the emasculation trend in the human species is the fact that the Right is also a whining coven of wenches. I forget the name of the teacher of rhetoric whose books I read at the Peabody Institute in 1999, but it began with a Q and he had already been dead for 1800 years and would have heartily approved of Vox Day's advice on how to form opinion. It is really a reminder that most of humanity is merely emotive and if thinkers want to touch them they need to be able to speak that low IQ, high-estrogen language.

When I clicked on this link I expected to find a discussion that white genocide does not work, but instead found a discussion about propaganda methods to preserve Western Culture. So, since Vox did not go there, I will.

The lands that became The United States were first colonized for the purpose of white genocide, and it failed. In the early 1600s, as Turkish warships were permitted to cruise the Irish Sea and English Channel unmolested by the greatest navy of the age, equipped with ships far more suited for the body of water than the Turkish galleys, as they raided for slaves, as many poor whites as possible were dumped on the shores of a primal land and used as slave labor, with every intention of working them to death. Females were only imported as replacement wives for the masters, the slaves barred from breeding, meant to die on that cruel westerly vine.

In the end, Civilization is intended to enslave the mass of every race in its place. Importing minority groups to destabilize an indigenous majority is a strategy as old as Akkad, Egypt and Assyria and beloved of the Incas.

But here we are, still alive.

The only thing that is needed for our kind to survive is for our men to remember to be men.

A True Man wakes with the dawn and the moon, knowing and accepting that enemies want his people, their stories, their memories to become the dust of oblivion. This is what it is to be a man in the primal sense—to know this.

The children of this man have a hope, a hope that may be extinguished by a single generation of false men.

The False Man, the civilized fool, believes that a political abstraction will enforce his fantasy of rights. He is the walker in a false dream, which is merely a traitor's suggested delusion that has but one deserved consequence, extinction.

The masters of this world weave a global web of lies meant to insure that the strong fall, the meek thrive and the weak spawn in a world become a hive.

The Goal of Civilization is the Death of Humanity and the Murder of God.

Thus far The Beast has done well.

Check out the cover for the Phillip K. Dick novel that was pulled.

https://voxday.blogspot.com/2016/05/why-whitegenocide-doesnt-work.html

'How Were People Racially Manipulated'

A Question from a Sociologist

"James, I see that you cited cases when whites and blacks fought together against the plantation aristocrats. Obviously, based on the divisive results, there was a method of separating the English slaves from the African slaves. Can you describe how this was accomplished?"

-Audrey

The Age Old Race Card

I can reconstruct the playing off of the various segments of the slave population against one another most completely in Virginia. Each colony [which was a charter for 'planting' people in plantations] had its own unique trajectory, with Maryland following a generation behind Virginia in most things. We are working from a mixed social base, as there was no policy of separating slaves by race known to be in force in Virginia from the 1620s-40s, when blacks were first introduced as slaves, indentured servants and freemen in very small numbers, ranging from 20-300 in all of Virginia, which had a population in excess of 10,000 through much of this period.

1. Black freemen could own black, Indian and mixed-race slaves, but not white slaves.

2. English speaking blacks from Barbados were segregated as house servants, with the English servants made to sleep in the barn with the livestock. This basic division would be maintained between House and Field once American servitude had become entirely a matter of managing blacks, and is maintained today between management and labor.

3. Once open mixed-race revolt occurred in 1676 free blacks were no longer permitted to go about armed and the following other measures were gradually enacted.

4. Increasing numbers of blacks were brought in at great expense as they had taken up arms against their masters at a rate of 10-20% whereas the English, Scottish and Irish slaves revolted at rates ranging from 30-70%.

5. Blacks were sought directly from Africa, so that there would be no common language to enable the lower classes to unite. The single best measure that a beleaguered elite can take against slave rebellion is to import lower class replacement labor who speak a different language from the indigenous servile population.

6. These slaves were quartered separately from the white slaves in segregated barracks.

7. These African slaves were sought to be as ethnically mixed as possible, in order to limit their cooperation across tribal and language barriers.

8. Where white slaves were denied the privilege of sex, and had their indentures extended and children sold, if caught, blacks, being expensive to ship, were

encouraged to reproduce on the plantation, causing poor whites to resent blacks as the favorites of their masters. It was more economic to replace white labor with kidnapped children from age 8-14, rather than nurture these creatures through an uncertain childhood. The financial burden of child servant rearing was such that whites indentured at birth had 31 year terms whereas those indentured at 14 had but 7 year terms. Blacks of course, expensive to ship, and not ready for work until age 5, were held for life [often abandoned to die of starvation in old age] in order to recoup the investment of childhood.

9. More white slaves were permitted to work off their indenture as opposed to being continually charged with crimes [such as eating when starved and crying when whipped] that would extend their term of service. The large scale slave economy dictated that such individuals, without property and assets and who had to carry freedom papers, were socially vulnerable and would have to seek employment with the

elite as overseers, supervising work they knew oh too well.

10. Free whites were forced by law and threat of indenture or fine, to act as slave-catchers.

11. In areas such as Maryland, where slave plantations were so dominant as to make a free living almost impossible, slave catchers were rewarded monetarily by statute and with advertised bonuses for the capture of any slave or servant of any race, which established a generally feeling of antipathy towards those held in bondage, who were increasingly black and mixed-race.

12. Restrictions on freedom for blacks were established, up to and including bans on masters freeing their own slaves.

13. The "one drop" rule, which determined that any person with more than a 1 in 17 parts sub-Saharan African ancestry was entirely black, served to preclude the rise of an intermediary mixed-race population [such as in Haiti] and continue racial polarization via the belief that African blood was a social

taint and that the spread of this moral corruption must be maintained by denying free or intermediary status to mixed-race people. This was done for the same reason and to the same effect as the current Leftist dogma that pure European ancestry constitutes an ineradicable moral taint, and may be cured by interbreeding.

14. Semantics developed to support ideas of servitude. Eventually the term "Negro" came to be understood as indicating an un-free person, followed by bondsmen and servant [which could be an un-free person of any race]. Slave was a term used with bitterness [in the same way "victim" is used today] among the un-free [black and white] to describe their condition, while the elite tended to avoid or minimize the use of this term until after Emancipation, at which point it was judiciously applied by the elite to indicate a formerly and exclusively black state of bondage.

Maintaining the division of the races into antagonistic force pools to be mobilized along the lines of opinion and belief shaped by the elites is a crucial aspect of domestic statesmanship. Where existing divisions are insufficient, diverse populations must be infused into the social strata to insure the necessary division of the Lower Will.

'What is Beautiful in Life?'

The Peace of Knowing an Ultimate Desire and the Sublime Thrill of Divine Sanction

This morning I sat on the back deck of the #55 bus to get a better view of the 4900 Block of Hazelwood Avenue, where five County palefaces have recently been attacked by immigrant hoodrats from the City. After refreshing my visual impression I fell asleep, and woke in the city at Overlea Station.

At Overlea Station, which, like the corner of Hazelwood and Kenwood is a Purge Marshaling Point, three black men and a woman, all ranging in age from their late 20s through early 30s, boarded, speaking loudly as they tramped up onto the back deck. They were dressed for some kind of work in khakis and blue polo shirts. The alpha male, a big silverback, then began to speak as to how white men who have the audacity to sit on the back deck will henceforth be treated.

1. White men who do not ask permission to sit on the back deck will be thrown off the bus.

2. White men who sit next to a black man instead of standing in the aisle, will be thrown out a window.

3. White men who smile will have the smile slapped from their face.

4. White men who do not apologize for boarding the bus will be beaten.

5. White men who sit on the back deck will be stomped by the entire group.

I was not addressed directly.

An 18-year-old white man, who ran and caught the bus was heckled by these adults, who directed the black, male bus driver not to let him board at this stop, but make him run to the next stop.

The driver did not comply and did wish me a "good, safe day" as the young white man cowered in the front of the bus.

Back in my prime I made certain to always sit on the back deck with the criminals—when I packed a knife and wanted to die by any random violent means that would take me away from this vile garden of lies.

A mature man, slowing, weakening—but armed again—I seek a more meaningful, more specific end.

I will henceforth always sit on the back deck, if there is room enough to seat my pale, narrow ass.

I have found myself fortunate, that a mere five days after my last stick-fight—my last possible life-affirming event—that I have finally arrived at my death wish.

I want to be slain by the partner of the pig I am eviscerating for attempting to avenge the decapitation of he who finally attempts to make good on such threats as uttered by the silverback above. Last year I ran from four predatory Negroes—never again.

After getting bruised up and having my fencing mask split fighting with Sean this past weekend, I thought I would never again experience beauty.

How wrong I was.

As I smiled up at my unworthy foe, I saw again that God provides for us all in some fitting way.

At 6:47, the bus pulled off and I walked down the middle of the street, blacker than that stupid ape will ever be.

At the crest of the first ridge, as the moon still hung grayly in the cloud-streaked morning sky, a crow on the light pole above flexed its wings and cawed once, angrily, I thought.

The thrill that animated me at that moment could have only been heightened if a rare and delicate flower would have sprung from the crack between the asphalt and the concrete there at Glenoak and Remmel, so that I might have crushed it under my boot.

Whether it takes a day or a decade, I have confidence in the truth of the omen and am content in embracing my Fate.

God does care.

'Men, Women, Children and Ancients'

Tecumseh: The Last Warrior (1995)

© 2016 James LaFond

Why the elites of European descent ever permitted working whites to cohabitate in their cities is beyond me. However, I suspect that what is depicted in this tepidly native-Centric view of the life of Panther-passing-across and the demise of his people, who migrated in stages across Pennsylvania and the Ohio valley for hundreds of years to avoid white conquest, could very well be the story of white flight. At least when the Shawnee [Summer-people] moved, they knew that the whites would be coming for them. The people being overrun by criminal mobs in the suburbs where I work, coach and travel, still do not understand that it is by design—that any master you run from will eventually send his slaves after you or yours.

https://www.youtube.com/watch?v=ohGiXsGWvgg

More Eirik Bloodaxe Via Kindle

Prepper Press Releases Zombie Apocalypse: Barbarians, Blades and Blood in the New Dark Age

Eirik, whose real name is Woden Nord Hammer, just emailed me to let the readers know that his second volume is up. Based on my reading of the manuscript he sent me, Volume Two is more about dealing with the Zombie hordes, whereas Volume One is essentially an explanation that the brain eaters are already among us.

Eirik has been busting his old Aussie ass on this, and it was already a major treasure in its raw form. So, based on his e-proofs, I'm recommending them.

As soon as my son downloads one of these kindle versions for me I'll review that.

Eirik, I can hardly believe this shit but the A-10 ground attack aircraft based at Martins Airfield are running at helicopter height over my humble abode—might the zombies already be massing?

Seriously, Uncle Bernie, if you're reading from your chair at the aviation museum, why the hell are these iron jockey's running so low over Hamilton—and more importantly, why are they not dropping their ordinance on this shithole!

The Death of a Race

A BBC Documentary on the Last Whites of an English Enclave

"Its chilling how this is almost exactly what is happening here, where you are, where I am. I think someone is getting fired at the BBC for this."

-Mescaline Franklin

Thank you, Mescaline, for this link.

When we combine guilt for the circumstances of your birth and the supposedly unforgivable sins of your ancestors, with an easy unfulfilling life, increasingly limited avenues of social advancement, erasure of gender, an astonishing supply of drugs provided by the so-called 'War on Drugs' and the utter abandonment of Man's innate desire to explore and burst the bounds imposed by his world, what you get is the Death of a Race. I am of the opinion that only a vast 90%+ cull of people of European descent could possible set the human race back on track to expand to the stars. Because, for some reason, the only race to ever break the bounds imposed by its world only does so against the odds, not when reclining in an environment wildly more lush than any Garden of Eden envisioned by early theologians.

In retrospect, the only purpose that poor whites ever had to the elite British was as cheap labor and cannon food. As long as the ranks can be filled with white soldiers, why would the British want any additional white people when labor is now exported to dedicated slave nations where less demanding races toil for the white elite?

Note in the conversation with the boxer, that he describes being threatened by three nonwhites and when he knocks them all out, they began charging him with the label of a racist.

https://www.youtube.com/watch?v=ZJ-D9atKl7Q#t=3464

Holding Out

Against the Criminals: a Man Question from Mescaline Franklin

"How could white guys hold out, fight back against the waves of criminals without getting plowed under by The State? I want to include women as a family residence effort— a real tribe."

-Mescaline Franklin

The answer is they cannot so long as the governing powers know that they exist. All of this tribalism and masculinity building, like The Wolves of Vinland, with membership based on criminal organizations, like biker clubs, is actually excellent for an insular fraternity developing quality men, but is total bullshit when it comes to effectively protecting loved ones, property, or even your own hairy hide, as the government will use the RICO statute to come after any fraternal organization that acts as a vigilante force.

It's just a fantasy—goddamned stupid.

As soon as you become, The Dogs or White Avenue, you are now the declared, surrounded, impeded, circumscribed, infinitely outnumbered enemy of the most powerful force that has trod the people of the Earth under foot.

I believe there is a way, a method that I had in mind for the story seed of Reverent Chandler, of how men of European descent, in this septic nation of sin, might someday reclaim their nature and fight back against the slathering beast that are the Dindu pet hordes of The State—a long shot, but a shot.

As for holding a neighborhood, unless you are all born there, how do you get there, unless you all go in and buy up an abandoned city block and gate it, which is an idea—except tat it is unsustainable, economically and legally. Attempts to build exclusive communities in rural areas draws the federal bloodhounds. Below are what I think must be The Principals of Conception for a community defense force.

1. Women must be excluded. Any wife or girlfriend, once threatened by authorities, will absolutely turn on her man for her children. And this is, after all, about the moral crime of birthing and raising white children. This is why the mafia always kept their women in the dark.

2. Their must be no organization, but a network of lone defenders.

3. Nothing may be written, in code or otherwise.

4. Nothing may ever be discussed electronically.

5. No defender may be admitted to the network unless he commits a crime against The State or one of its criminal pets. Wrecking a transformer at a national guard armory or shanking a drug dealer would be good examples.

6. Firearms use would be limited as The State is so well versed in tracing firearms crime.

7. No uniforms, colors, slogans, signs, or any indication that an action was a group action should be employed. This must be a ghost-like undertaking.

8. The focus of the defenders should be eliminating criminals, or their presence, one at a time.

9. There can be no financial facet of the group, with self-sustaining actions by defenders marking a strictly delineated danger zone for thugs—the criminals will figure out your operational zone, so there is no sense in declaring it, unless a verbal warning about a violent third party—not a threat from you, a concerned citizen just looking out for the panhandler's safety—for a minor criminal seems prudent.

10. Professional criminals, such as police, gang members, bikers, drug dealers, etc., should not be recruited. They have no souls

and no honor and will, always and absolutely, betray the defenders.

11. Defenders should join church groups, and find a way to tap into the neighborhood watch facebook postings in the operational zone, using a woman for this.

12. The primary activity of defenders should be intelligence gathering.

13. Defenders should speak out against violent action and vigilante activity to anyone who would listen.

14. Verbalization to targeted criminals should be strictly banned. It is ineffective and incriminating.

Keep in mind that criminals are very easy to hit. Uniformed cops are usually idiots and they grab thugs all of the time. Stupid teenage girls manage to kill thugs by the vanload, so you can certainly break a leg and give the victim a look.

Good like finding such men. Our society is structure to preclude their development.

I intend to write a novel about such a resistance movement, titled Paleface.

For the record, this discussion was for informational purposes only, is a bad idea, and should never be attempted. I for one avoid joining any organization for any purpose. And will only act violently to defend or avenge myself or loved ones, not to defend some false notion such as community solidarity.

Comments

» Add a comment «

PR   June 1, 2016 11:56 PM EDT

This is a plan William Lind would approve of. It lacks a propaganda arm, though.

Are beatings of criminals enough for them to get the point, or to you have to bludgeon them with something or use a knife?

It would probably be could to keep criminals guessing as to what your operational zone was. Raids into criminal territory might be a good idea.

Guest   June 1, 2016 7:25 AM EDT

I also like how it's exactly 14 points, 14

points for 14 words.

"14 Words" is a reference to the most popular white supremacist slogan in the world: "We must secure the existence of our people and a future for white children." according to the ADL.

What an evil and supremacist notion!
Guest   May 31, 2016 8:18 PM EDT

Even a trilogy perhaps? Bet on it, The Walking Black & Paleface! They could be informally known as the PPP, the pale penis people! This is a term the Z Man mockingly uses (and coined it).

The Sword of 'Yo-Damocles'

The Problem with Propaganda: Afterword to Paleface Sunset

The question of "a propaganda arm" for Caucasian crime resistors has been suggested in response to my recent musing on how men might protect their neighborhood in a world where crime against individuals is essentially sanctioned. This is not solely an interracial phenomenon. This is primarily a question of Asians, Whites and Blacks [Latinos have this down] defending themselves against blacks, for the black underclass in America has been successfully cultivated as a violent mob, a sword of "Yo-Damocles" if you will.

Yes, whenever a black thug is stopped by a white man, the white man—law officer or not—is lynched in the media and investigated and sometimes charged by law enforcement. The "black lives matter" movement is only concerned with persecuting those who oppose the government-backed, black mob, not with the innocent blacks they routinely violate, with no media or government notice being taken.

Recently two elderly, Baltimore City, black women have been beaten, raped, tortured and robbed by young black men in their homes! The police did post these crimes. However, the media decided not to follow up on either one of these stories, declining to even report the rape that was not fatal. The woman in her 90s died. The 71-year-old woman was in such a rage she walked herself to the Channel 2 News station and reported the crime herself! The media has a vested interest in covering up such things, for they are slaves to the political class and eat from the table of State.

This brings us to the question of propaganda.

Propaganda is an emotive form of communication, guaranteed to arouse emotional personalities to action. Not clearly thinking tactical actors with strategic vision, but bullies and boisterous demagogues have ever been the target and purveyor of such propaganda. When such a man—necessarily as much woman as man—gains the social gavel, the very characteristics that make him a rouser to action, a shaper of opinion, will disqualify him for the rational execution of the duties of the leadership position his politicking shall earn for him.

For instance, right now, the media and politicians deny black-on-white crime and blame black-on-black crime on whites. The sole purposes is to persecute whites as, thus far in history, people of European descent have been the most troublesome to rule. The begging, whining and constant self-killing of blacks only seems to be troublesome if one falsely believes that The State exists to serve The People. If one understands that The State exists to exploit The People, then these criminals and greedy consumers become useful to those in actual power. For one thing, it makes those aware whites think that this condition is a matter of race, and that if only The State is strengthened by their people, things will be as they should be. This is a symptom of reactionary thinking, which is purely emotive—a mirrored misunderstanding of the nature of POWER.

For the past 30 years Left wing secularists have doggedly pursued priests and ministers for raping altar boys and other people under their power. Recently, citing the fact that The Left operates behind the Lie, numerous New Right thinkers have concluded that no altar boys were ever raped, that religious figures have been persecuted because they are an anchor of The Right. Such misunderstanding is generated by the necessary simple messages of propaganda. The fact is, that Christianity, in the Western Experience, is The Old Left, and these institutions have been under constant assault by the New Left so that their secular ideology might replace the many-candled Church that was the original communist movement in the Western Experience. All learning institutions, including secular schools and religions, are fertile ground for sex criminals interested in exploiting the young. So, when it was time to change ideological foundations on The Left, the actors knew where to look for real persecution-worthy crimes to assist in their dismantling of the Church.

Based on how the rulers of this nation have successfully played racial and ethnic groups off against each other since 1609, I see propaganda on black-on-white crime missing the point that it is government sanctioned and therefore appealing primarily to emotive types who will make regularly predictable miscalculations, and at best, continue to power the racial see-saw that keeps the invisible elite secure behind closed minds.

In terms of men acting to defend their community against the current government-sponsored violence of black thugs—and against the Islamic rape squads that will be hunting the remains of this nation in 20 years, with government sanction, as they now do in Europe—I prefer having them isolated from the production or transmittance of propaganda. Also, propaganda that goes beyond the ethos of defending your own against any and all threats, according to the most effective means available, must not be traced to an actor, lest he be successfully prosecuted. Even such ideals as simple family and neighborhood defense should only be spoken man to man, the only context in which the proper masculine actor will ever be recruited. Defenders of their community should be isolated from any words espousing the crime of defending against The Mob.

Defenders of community and family must learn from their enemies, that just as a criminal avoids conviction by employing lawyers, they should not ever speak of their commitment beyond the small circle of men they stand with and that others, with no provable connection with them, might speak on their behalf and in terms with only one objective, preserving their freedom to act, not imbuing it with a motive that may then be used to persecute and prosecute them for the ultimate crime in tomorrow's America— defending family.

Understand that your family is the ultimate target, the thing that must be destroyed to arrive at a single social mind.

It is no accident that currently, the ethnic group that enjoys the highest level of government preference has no family structure. Currently, black urban households are either single-mother, or no parent, with a handful of two parent anomalies and a growing percentage of "no grandparent" households, in which a great grandmother or aunt or foster mother serves as a shepherd into what may well become Humanity's longest night.

Understand that, like a zombie or vampire movie, that those who attack you have long ago been reduced to the terrible, soulless fate that they now instinctively seek to visit upon you.

The End

Made in the USA
Monee, IL
21 October 2021